A Bromsgrove Carpenter's Tale

The early life and times of
Arthur James 1878-1914

A Bromsgrove Carpenter's Tale

The early life and times of
Arthur James 1878-1914

Introduced and edited
by
Margaret Cooper

Foreword by Michael Gill
Chairman, Bromsgrove District Council

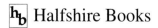 Halfshire Books

First published in Great Britain by
Halfshire Books
130 New Road, Bromsgrove
Worcestershire B60 2LE

Copyright © 2001 Gordon James

ISBN 1 899062 06 8

Printed and bound in Great Britain by
Bookcraft, Midsomer Norton, Bath

Contents

List of photographs

Foreword

Reading the recollections of Arthur James, together with the additional notes, reminds us how much Bromsgrove has changed in the last hundred years, some would say out of all recognition. At the same time we can probably recognise the people who make their appearance in his story, not by name necessarily but certainly by personality: the fun-loving, the miserable, the generous, the mean-spirited, the risk-takers, the cautious, the stiff-upper-lips, the hang-it-all-outs. People don't really change.

Is our town a much better place now? Even those who look back with longing to 'the good old days' will find that this book dispels some illusions about the quality of life at the end of the nineteenth and beginning of the twentieth century. Huge problems, such as the extreme poverty of a significant proportion of the population, lack of decent housing, a traditional industry in headlong decline and an almost total absence of effective public health measures, have been the subject of much national and local government legislation and largely eradicated. Not many would want to turn the clock back so far. On the other hand, just as there never was a 'golden age' so there probably never will be, and perhaps it is true to say that Bromsgrovians face a different set of problems today in a world which is very much more complex and hectic.

Arthur James was the son of a nail manufacturer whose family was better off than those of many of his schoolmates. He describes the poverty of the late-nineteenth century which was so typical of the children of nailmakers whose families were just trying to eke out an existence in any way they could. In Arthur's account of his education we get some of the horrors of Victorian discipline, epitomised in the old phrase 'spare the rod and spoil the child'. But we also get some of the fun and the good times, and the rigours of school life provided Arthur and his friends with a grounding which was to stand them in good stead for later life. A number of these children, who would now be classified as deprived, went on to become real achievers.

Our great concern today for all aspects of community health is a marked contrast to yesteryear's when public hygiene was virtually non-existent. The very thought of the visits of the night soil men is good enough reason to shudder. One can only feel a great sadness at the loss of so many lives, both old and young, from the kind of diseases which no longer threaten us.

It is interesting to note that although nailmaking was dying out in the four decades recalled by Arthur James it has been replaced by many and varied trades for the men and women of Bromsgrove and by the establishment of businesses in the town which are household names.

The identification of so many of the characters who touched the lives of the James family and played their respective parts in the everyday life of Bromsgrove adds considerably to the memoirs themselves. For those familiar with the geography of the town this book is a mine of fascinating detail about the buildings and the people who lived and worked in them, and I have little doubt that the mention of some of the names will bring back memories of folk and families long forgotten – including Joseph Tilt who built the former Council House, kept the Hop Pole and was elected to the Urban District Council.

The town may have grown immensely since Arthur's days, but I can recommend this book – with its vivid descriptions and well-researched additional information – to the newcomer as well as to the native Bromsgrovian.

Michael Gill, Chairman, Bromsgrove District Council

Preface

Gordon James had no idea his father had spent over a year writing down some of his earlier memories until he sorted through his papers shortly after his death in 1963. Had he known about the recollections he would certainly have encouraged Arthur to carry on with them and bring his story up to date. Instead, he was left wondering why they had come to such a sudden halt.

From time to time Arthur records the date of writing, so that we know he had started by August 1949, was halfway through by the following February, and was getting towards the end of his manuscript in August 1950. By this time his wife Ethel was already showing the early signs of Alzheimer's disease and in 1951 was admitted to Barnsley Hall where she died four years later. It may be that very different priorities caused Arthur to lose interest in his project. We shall probably never know.

Arthur William James was born on 3 December 1878 in Walton Road, Norton, Bromsgrove, and died on 3 August 1963 at the age of eighty-four. His father and grandfather were both in the nailing industry which, though in long decline, still in the last decades of the nineteenth century employed considerable numbers in the area. Arthur, however, went to school, did well there and became a pupil teacher. But a year was long enough to convince him that teaching was not his future and at the age of fourteen he was apprenticed as a carpenter and joiner to William Weaver, the builder.

One of the most significant events in Arthur's life occurred in 1908 when the body of his father John was found in Pikes Pool. An inquest recorded a verdict of 'Found Drowned'. Arthur, the main witness and then in his late twenties, was devastated by the way his father had died and a serious breakdown followed. Eventually he did recover and lived on into his eighties, but he never really got over the tragedy.

When he began his recollections Arthur was in his early seventies. Had he gone on writing he might well have said something about the demise of the old building firm of Tilt Bros in the difficult years before the Second World War; the day-to-day life in Bromsgrove during those war years; and the local reaction to some of the great social changes introduced immediately after the war. He recorded enough, however, to leave behind some vivid glimpses of everyday life in the area in the late- nineteenth century. What makes them of special interest is their focus on the northern end of the town where a growing population led to the creation of a new parish in the 1880s and a new urban district in the following decade.

North Bromsgrove was a community full of characters, many of them nailers with colourful (and 'politically incorrect') nicknames, a few offering age-old services such as rabbit catching and herbal advice. It was a community whose children attended the new Board schools, though 'attended' might be too emphatic a word for the irregular appearances put in by some of the pupils. It was a community - like several others in Bromsgrove - which included families in extreme poverty who, at the worst of times, queued up at soup kitchens for 'halfpenny dinners' provided by kind ladies. It was a community where cockerels, chickens, even peacocks, took possession of the main Birmingham Road. And it was a community that loved its music.

Arthur's son Gordon served a seven-year apprenticeship in wood and stone carving with Austrian-born Celestino Pancheri who had broken away the Bromsgrove Guild in 1926 and had set up with A W Hack in a workshop next to the butcher's in Aston Fields. Two years into his training Gordon was joined by Celestino's son Robert who was the same age but had stayed on at Bromsgrove School until he was sixteen.

At the start of his apprenticeship there seemed to be plenty of work. Gordon remembers Celestino employing no less than ten woodcarvers for a whole year on a commission in a church in Wolverhampton; but by the time he finished his apprenticeship in 1936 the situation had changed and shortly afterwards he was made redundant. For a couple of years or so Gordon moved backwards and forwards between Pancheri and Eddie Dean, another ex-Guild member, who had set up as a monumental mason in Sidemoor and worked for the Guild on a contractual basis; but when the war broke out Gordon moved to Longbridge, where he made model patterns for the tools used to manufacture aeroplane frames.

The young men in the pattern shop were keen to join up, but their work was considered too important, and despite several attempts Gordon didn't finally get the call until 1945 'when it was practically all over!'. He went back to Longbridge a couple of years later to make model patterns, this time for car engine tools, and there he stayed until his retirement. He had, however, kept up his carving skills in his leisure time and so was able to answer some calls for help from his old fellow apprentice Robert Pancheri. In 1987, for example, operating in their separate workshops, the two men restored much of the elaborate carving in the Tower of the Four Winds, a folly in the grounds of Shugborough Hall in Staffordshire.

For greater convenience the explanatory notes have been placed as far as possible alongside the main text rather than at the back of the book.

When Arthur James started school this was the new Board School, built on land called the Meadows in Stourbridge Road. Nearly 120 years later there are still spiked railings and the boys' entrance is a reminder of the strict division

Introduction

1 1878

Arthur James was born during a hard winter. The first snowstorm hit
the town on 24 November, ten days before his arrival, and it proved
to be a herald of what was to come. The weather that year had
already produced a number of extreme fronts. Early January was so
mild that Mr Corbett, the High Street chemist, had found a fully
developed stag butterfly, and three weeks later Mr Rose, the sexton,
had come upon another 'beautiful butterfly' (both discoveries
faithfully reported in the *Bromsgrove Messenger*). In early August
four days of heavy thunderstorms had caused the town's brook to
rise to an 'extraordinary height'; but a month later a brilliant spell, a
really hot Indian summer, had proved a tremendous boon for the
farmers. In mid-November, just before the onset of the very cold
period, Bromsgrove had been lucky to escape the worst effects of
exceptionally heavy rain which had caused serious flooding at
Droitwich, Feckenham and Alcester.

Along with Bromsgrove's other residents that yearArthur's
parents were invited to take an interest in the designation and, later,
the consecration of the new Bishop of Newfoundland (a former
curate at St John's), and to celebrate the coming-of-age of Lord
Windsor by roasting a couple of oxen in the town centre. There may
have been more reaction to the report of the purchase of two cows
and three heifers by Henry Allsopp, MP for East Worcestershire.
The five animals cost £11,000, only £500 less than the 72-acre
Warwick Hall estate which was sold some months later.

This was the year when two men were acquitted of highway
robbery at Stoke Prior, when two others were given four months'

The coffee house opened in the High Street just before Christmas 1878. It was a local initiative, but part of a national temperance movement which aimed to offer an alternative to alcohol. Bromsgrove's coffee tavern soon became a branch of the County and City of Worcester Coffee Tavern Company and clearly sold the famous Melton Mowbray pies as well as non-alcoholic beverages.

hard labour, one for stealing clothes, the second for escaping from
Worcester gaol, and when a man called Hall received twelve
months' hard labour for stealing some table knives from the Dolphin
Inn.

It was the year that the bishop of Worcester confirmed 282 people
(from St John's and surrounding parishes) at Bromsgrove's old
parish church on the last Sunday in April; that the go-ahead
publican at the nearby Golden Cross established a public billiard
table, the only one for miles around; and that just before Christmas a
public coffee house was opened in the Hight Street as part of the
national temperance movement.

More significantly, in 1878 the Cottage Hospital, five converted
cottages, was opened on New year's Day at Mount Pleasant, the
name given to the hill on Stratford Road; the nailers – some of them
working for Arthur's grandfather - were out on strike again, this
time for a month; and just days before Arthur was born the
Bromsgrove School Board agreed to buy a site on the Stourbridge
Road for a new Board school.

2 The James family

Arthur James came from nailing stock. His grandfather George and
his father John worked together from their warehouse in
Birmingham Road (formerly the newsagent's below Barnsley
Road). They stored the iron there, handing out the rods to the nailers
and paying them when the nails were brought in at the end of the
week. So they knew the nailing community well; but they were
'gaffers', better off than the men and women they employed, and it
is clear from Arthur's remarks that moving to New Buildings when
he was eight years old was something of a social step down. On the
other hand, it is also clear from the warmth with which he writes
about those years that Arthur had some very good times with the
friends he made there.

John James married Emma Tandy of Kenilworth in 1869. He was
twenty and she was two years younger. They had four children:
John (Jack), Amy, Arthur and Dora. Jack died in the 1887 typhoid
outbreak when he was sixteen and training to be a teacher. By that
stage he was already an accomplished organist. Amy, five years

older than Arthur, became a schoolteacher and, blessed with some of her father's musical talent, was well known in the area as a singer and music teacher. Dora, nine years Arthur's junior, was the violinist in the family, again taught by her father. She was much the quieter of the sisters, looking after Amy when the latter was widowed and in ill health, and then after Amy's son Leonard who never married. John James senior was never really happy as a nail manufacturer. He seems to have been a caring and sensitive man with genuine sympathy for the plight of the nailers, uncomfortable, in particular, about the way they were short-changed by many of the manufacturers and 'foggers' (the middlemen). Besides, music was his real passion and in a later age his talent would probably have provided him with a living.

John's tragic death at the age of fifty-six cast a long shadow over Arthur's life. According to reports in the *Bromsgrove Messenger* his father left his home in New Buildings at 8.30 am on Saturday 21 March 1908 to make one of his usual business journeys to the Black Country. When he failed to return the next day his family became anxious, particularly as he had not been well, and contacted the police. On the following Wednesday, having been told that John had been seen in the vicinity of Pikes Pool around midday on the Saturday looking 'very ill', PC Beavan searched the area without success. On the following day, with the help of George Empson of Finstall, he took a boat out to drag the pool. The two men found John's body, fully dressed, with spectacles, pipe, tobacco and 10d in his pockets, and removed it to Finstall village hall where the inquest was held on the following day.

It is clear that the deputy coroner, Mr A H Herbert, was trying to discover whether there was any evidence for a suicide verdict. There were some hints. Arthur, the surviving son and main witness, had been with his father two days before his disappearance. He didn't think his father would have attempted suicide, but he confirmed that John had been in poor health, having suffered from bronchitis and asthma for ten years. He had also been very depressed and Arthur suspected he was short of money - he had been saying for some time that his business was worth very little. And both PC Beavan and George Empson suggested that any man accidentally falling down the bank of the pool could easily have saved himself.

The jury, however, perhaps reluctant to bring in a verdict that in those days would have brought shame and distress to the family, returned one of 'Found Drowned', having heard no evidence to support suicide nor any to show how John had come to be in the pool. The foreman did venture to remark that some jury members felt a more adequate fence should be provided between the road and the pool, but the deputy coroner reminded them that this 'had been thrashed out before' - owners could not be compelled to fence their land except to keep cattle in, and this was a question for the parish council.

Arthur makes no reference to his wife and children in the recollections that follow, but we know that he was just twenty-two when he married Ethel Merriman at All Saints Church on 24 December 1900. Ethel, three years younger, was the daughter of George Merriman, the first superintendent engineer at the East Worcestershire Waterworks Company's Burcot works, and was born and brought up in the company's house. To start with, the newlyweds lived on the opposite side in one of a row of three cottages known as The Mount; then they moved briefly to All Saints Road where Hilda, their first child, was born, and then to Norton Villas where they had a second daughter Phyllis and two sons, William and, five years later in 1916, Gordon. William followed in his maternal grandfather's footsteps, becoming the engineer at the Burcot works and then superintendent at the Washing Stocks works. He moved on to South Staffordshire, then Normanton in Nottinghamshire where the engines were driven, not by diesel as in Worcestershire, but by steam.

3 A new parish

The ecclesiastical parish of All Saints was carved out of St John's on 14 May 1875 in response to the increase in population. The parish stretched up the Birmingham Road as far as the tollgate above the original vicarage, down into the High Street to the northern side of Mill Lane, across to the northern edge of Sidemoor and up the Stratford Road. The church was already in place, built between 1872 and 1874 of local stone and at a cost of £5,600. The organ, installed in 1875, cost a further £420 but this was paid for

This photograph of the wedding of Florence Merriman to Bertram Moore in the late 1890s was taken in the garden of the Waterworks House in Burcot. Arthur James is on the back row, extreme right; Ethel - shortly to be his wife – is next to the bride, her sister; Ethel's parents, George and Emily, stand behind the bride and groom.

These are Gordon James's two grandmothers: on the left is Emma James, nee Tandy, who married Gordon's grandfather John in 1869, and on the right is Emily Merriman whose daughter Ethel married Gordon's father Arthur in 1900.

Emily Merriman and her mother, known as 'Granny Spires', were both outworkers for a needle firm in Redditch. Using a small hammer Emily would knock out any minor blemishes to ensure that the needles were absolutely straight. Granny Spires would then count the needles into twelves, put them into pre-folded paper and seal each packet with a gummed label.

Emily's husband George, the waterworks manager, noticed one day how the labels provided by the needle firm tended to stick together; so he went off to his workshop and devised a special tool of very thin metal which made separating the sticky labels very much easier. His mother-in-law carried on as an outworker until her death.

Granny Spires is seated on the extreme right in the previous photograph (her husband is on the extreme left). Her daughter Emily stands behind the bride and her thoughtful son-in-law behind the groom.

entirely by public subscription. All 618 sittings in the pews were free, in marked contrast to arrangements at St John's where nearly half were still being 'rented'. In 1883 a large Sunday School was added and five years later the tower which has become one of the main features in Bromsgrove's landscape.

Rev the Hon Adolphus Henry Turthill Massey MA of Trinity College, Dublin, was the first vicar, a high churchman who stayed for twenty years despite the comparatively modest living of £282. (St John's was worth £650.) He was described by a former parishioner as tall, spare and rather fragile-looking, but he was clearly stronger than he appeared. He played a particularly energetic game of tennis and in a vivid little episode once put muscular Christianity into action by jumping from his carriage in Bromsgrove, seizing hold of a man who was attacking a woman and depositing him in the gutter. Rev Massey was succeeded by Rev Francis Lea Milward MA of Christ's College, Cambridge. The living had not increased but congregations and Sunday School attendance continued to be very high, suggesting that the people of North Bromsgrove had happily made the move from the old parish church to the new.

In 1894 the old town and district boards were replaced under the new Local Government Act by two urban district councils for Bromsgrove and North Bromsgrove. The latter district included Bournheath, Catshill, Lickey End, Sidemoor, Linthurst and Worms Ash, and the new board met at 4.30 pm on the first Tuesday of every month. George James, probably John's brother, was an influential member and, for several years, its chairman.

Arthur was born over the road from Townsend Farm where 'Weaver the Milkman', father of the founder of Bromsgrove's most successful building firm, set out each day on his delivery round with his horse and shoulder yoke and spotlessly clean white smock, measuring out the milk at each door. A little further up was Bridgman's flour mill and the pool where children (for a small fee) were allowed to bathe.

When he was eight Arthur moved to New Buildings, a row of small terraced cottages built between two 'foredraughts', or paths, both leading through to the Stourbridge Road. Top Foredraught was opposite the Crab Mill, and Lower Foredraught, high-hedged and more private, ran roughly along the line of Victoria Road.

George Byng, the father of Fred, Arthur's great pal, was a very successful florist. This photograph of Hollyville in All Saints Road appeared in the particulars of an auction held in July 1907 at the Golden Cross Hotel when Byng was selling up to concentrate entirely on his Churchfields site. His substantial three-storey 'villa residence' included five bedrooms and several touches of luxury - a fitted bath, gas and tap water, and an elaborate west-facing verandah.

   Curiously, Byng was also selling the goodwill of the business, 'The New Town Nurseries' (which appeared, probably for the first time, in a local advert in 1900). But 1907 was the year he added to his advert the phrase 'Acknowledged by Royalty' and confidently claimed to be the area's leading florist, so he was obviously not worried about any New Town competition. The family business operated in Churchfields for most of the century.

The land over which the foredraughts passed was bought at the beginning of the 1880s by Bromsgrove and Stoke Prior Building Society and then balloted in lots among the society's members. This led to the immediate building of two new roads, Victoria and All Saints, and to new houses. The area was called New Town Estate (New Town Villas, a row of four terraced houses in Victoria Road, still bear witness to this development), but the community went on calling the new roads 'top' and 'lower'. All Saints Road was intended for shops but a certain Mr G K Stanton ignored the society's rules and built two houses halfway along. Others soon followed suit.

4 Stourbridge Road Board School

Shortly before Arthur was born the Bromsgrove School Board, established in 1875 following the 1870 Education Act, agreed to pay £657.19.0 for a site at the Meadows on the Stourbridge Road in order to build another school. Two Board schools had already opened in 1877, one at Lickey End (to accommodate 255 children) and one at Dodford (to accommodate 144 children). Stourbridge Road was much the biggest, able to take 200 boys, 200 girls and 100 'mixed' infants. The joint bid from Jonathan Brazier and William Weaver of £3,563.10.0 was once again the most competitive (they had already built the Lickey End and Dodford schools) and the building, designed by Messrs E A Day and F J Yates, was ready for the children by November 1880.

The Boys' Department consisted of three rooms: the main room (68.5 ft x 20 ft), the West classroom (22.5 ft x 20 ft) and the North classroom (19 ft x 20 ft), and here the 200 (in theory) were taught. The Girls' Department, under the headship of Miss Jane Mitchell, was almost identical in size and layout. The 100 mixed infants were squeezed into two rooms, the larger only half the size of the boys' and girls' main rooms.

Arthur probably started as a 'mixed infant' when he was five but we can't be certain: schools could accept children long before that age - and at any stage of the term and on any day of the week. In charge was Miss Ellen Hooper, the only qualified teacher. She was assisted (and probably sometimes hindered) by three pupil teachers at various stages of their training. The most senior, Mary Roberts, had begun as a monitress when the school opened and in late 1873 would have been starting the fourth of her five-year training. She was barely seventeen. Minnie Wildsmith was in her third year and Miss H E Clews just beginning her second.

Arthur's references to the teachers in the Boys' School - especially to Mr Stanton – are very interesting. Shortly after Arthur's upward move Charles Hayward, the headmaster, left to take up a headship in Birmingham. He was succeeded in September 1886 by Charles Fletcher, until then head at Catshill Board School. Both men were certificated teachers (having done the pupil-teacher training *and* then gone on to college) as was the senior assistant Mr E Badger. Frederick Martin had qualified at the end of 1884 via a five-year apprenticeship at Hanbury National School; but Levett Nokes and Ernest Stanton did not finish their pupil-teacher training until October 1889. So Arthur's Grade 5 teacher Mr Stanton, the 'great burly fellow … nicknamed Bull Head' of whom he was clearly in awe, just about eighteen and just about qualified.

A year earlier it hadn't looked at all certain that Ernest would get that far. According to the inspector's annual report his grasp of history, maths and teaching methods left a lot to be desired; and later the headmaster felt compelled to record in the school logbook that Stanton was still very 'backward' in his studies. His attendance at the special lessons set apart for his instruction was irregular and he did his home lessons 'by fits and starts'. The head went so far as to write down his worst fears: he might end his apprenticeship as unsatisfactorily as his two predecessors had. So Mr Fletcher resolved to give him as much extra help as he could. His faith in this particular pupil-teacher was well rewarded. By 1891 twenty-year-old Ernest Stanton was senior assistant, in charge on the odd days when the head was out and about.

The two teenage trainees who had made such a mess of things were Edward Buckingham and John Perrygrove. Both failed their third year training in 1886. Buckingham (often 'unaccountably absent') was suspended for a short time in 1887, while Perrygrove's lax behaviour in and out of school caused grief both to the head and his father. The boys failed again in 1887 and at that point disappear from the school's records; but Perrygrove made a triumphant return, having trained elsewhere, and was appointed assistant teacher in 1894. By 1900 he was senior assistant and 'after an absence of four-and-a-half years with the Colours' resumed duties in April 1919. He was still there when Gordon James was a pupil in the 1920s, by now a strong disciplinarian with a commanding military bearing.

Oliver Eades was another headache for Mr Fletcher. He failed his second year in 1887; but he kept going and qualified in 1892 (shortly after Arthur left), though only after two attempts at his final exam.

Two of Arthur's 'teachers', William Duffill and Frank Jeffrey, were even further down the scale, mere monitors, probably twelve or thirteen years old when Arthur moved up into the Boys' School. Monitors were older pupils employed to teach the most basic lessons to younger children, in theory under supervision. They were extremely cheap (usually £6 a year) and in the main extremely inefficient, and many didn't progress any further. Both William and Frank failed the annual inspection in 1886 and didn't last very much longer at the school. In fact 1886 was not the best of years: four of the five pupil teachers failed the diocesan exam on religious education.

Every school had trouble with monitors and pupil-teachers. There was nothing unusual about Stourbridge Road's record. On the contrary, despite these difficulties, reports of the annual inspections usually included a great deal of praise for the work going on in the school, and there seems to have been an acknowledgement that this was especially commendable in view of the social problems in the catchment area. Trouble inevitably went hand in hand with the set-up. The trainees were teenagers, having to attend before and/or after the day's work for individual study. And all this for a pittance, even less than they could have earned as nailers.

The children, too, could make life hard for the headmaster; but a word must be put in here for young Arthur Wheeler, since he is no longer able to defend himself. In 1891 stone throwing was a particular cause for concern – not just in this school but at others and in the town as a whole. Mr Fletcher had worked hard to eliminate it on his patch but was forced to record that the practice had been 'nearly wiped out except for Arthur Wheeler'.

But Arthur, much mentioned in log-book despatches, was not the only naughty boy. Thomas Leadbetter, for example, a member of a much respected family, was punished for using 'very abusive language'; an eight-year-old pinched a classmate's hat (though the local sergeant was on the case the very same day); and there were many others who bunked off, threw stones and didn't pay attention.

5 School attendance

Board schools faced many problems and with the best will in the world it was hard for the staff, many very young and inexperienced, to cope. Classes were huge (often more than twice the size of today's) and equipment poor or non-existent. The level of poverty affected not only how often but in what state the children turned up to school; and it didn't help that many remained unconvinced about the need to provide an elementary education for all children.

All Saints Church in about 1906. For many years the house stood in front of the west entrance, its owner persistently refusing to sell. Eventually it was bought and demolished, enabling Alfred Tilt to build and donate the lychgate in memory of his father Joseph.

In the first week of July 1887, for example, average attendance at the Boys' School was only 152 out of the 225 on the registers. In the last week of May 1890 it was even worse, down to 57%. Several factors contributed to the irregular appearance of so many children. The most significant was hardship. The school drew on a very impoverished area, many of its pupils from poor nailing families, and it was a long time before some parents were able to resist keeping their children off school in order to work at the nailblock or do the washing or look after the baby - in one way or another adding vital pennies to desperately low incomes. Those who were keen to send their children to school couldn't always afford the school pence or even the clothes to get them there.

One literally down-to-earth obstacle was footwear. Some children's boots and shoes couldn't cope with bad weather or the poor roads and paths. The school did its best to help and in 1889 opened a Children's Shoe Club, in effect a savings club; but the teachers also organised special concerts and the money raised provided direct assistance for the neediest of the needy. Poorly housed and badly nourished children were also more prone to illness and disease, and at this stage children were still dying from whooping cough, scarlet fever, diarrhoea, typhoid and measles.

Nor did legislation help. When Arthur went to school most children had to stay on until their thirteenth birthday, but could leave as early as ten if they had passed Standard 5. Once children had passed Standard 4, however, and provided they were over ten years of age, they were required to attend for only two hours a day and allowed to work for half the day. But a number didn't keep the school attendance part of the bargain. Mr Hayward complained in his logbook in December 1884 that the half-time work by William Wall and George Holland at the button factory was not at all conducive to learning.

Then of course there were those children who just didn't want to go to school. It's not difficult to sympathise. The state had sprung a new law on them and the idea of having to sit in school every day for at least five and very possibly eight years must have taken some getting used to. And school conditions were very basic: bad weather, for instance, could mean wet clothes all day; bad behaviour certainly did mean some sort of physical punishment. Worst of all, children who didn't pass the yearly exams were kept down until they did. How must they have felt, sitting in a class of younger - sometimes much younger - children? For the reluctant learner none of this looked encouraging.

Besides, there were other customs and other attractions. Try as he did - and one year he re-jigged the summer holiday dates - the headmaster didn't stand a chance when it came to seasonal activities. In July there was pea picking, in late August the harvest, in early autumn (sometimes for five weeks!) there was hop picking, and a little later potatoes took centre stage. These were traditional family-based activities providing much vital income. Then there were exciting events like the visiting circus and the annual June fair, and one-off occasions like the visit of the Shah of Persia. Sensibly, the children were given the day off for such high days - but some of them always added on the days either side. Even Sunday School treats affected attendance since these usually occurred on week days.

Irregular attendance had, as one annual report described, 'an evil effect' on the school. Lesson plans were ruined and the school's grant reduced because this was based not only on exam results but also on attendance figures. At times Mr Fletcher despaired, sent long lists of names to the attendance officer, urged the School Board to take action against the parents. But for a long time the Board was reluctant to act and as late as 1890 the headmaster noted that although a few parents had been prosecuted some Board members were still not keen to enforce the bye-laws.

The head's frustration is understandable, but so, to some extent, is the Board's ambivalence. Many families desperately needed the small amount of money their children could earn, a situation which could make the attendance officer's job quite dangerous; and even when prosecution was pursued the magistrate, recognising poverty, would often impose a fine smaller than the amount the child could earn if the parents chose to defy the authorities.

6 Blind Jack

Blind Jack, as he was widely known, is mentioned several times in the memoirs and was a very well known figure in the Bromsgrove area. Jack (christened John) was the son of William Wakeman, a shopkeeper and gardener, and Louisa, a nailer. He was born in 1862 or 1863 and an anonymous contributor to *The Messenger* remembered Jack as a fellow scholar in the 1860s at a small dame school run by Miss Emma Price, the invalid sister of the headmistress of the National Girls' School. Jack wasn't totally blind at that stage but by the time he was eighteen he was following the trade of basket making, a very common occupation amongst blind people.

Jack delivered papers for Rea's, the newsagents next to The Mitre, and in 1991 Ruth Rea, who had often accompanied him on his rounds when she was a girl, described him as a 'marvellous man', quick to get the feel of a route and sometimes doing it on his own.

The tragic accident which Arthur James mentions (see page 65) happened on Monday, 11 December 1911 at a time, 4.20 pm, when the light was already fading. The little boy involved was, according to the inquest report, Jack's nephew, Jack Norbury, the four-year-old son of Mr and Mrs Joseph Norbury of Vine Cottage in Birmingham Road. In the car, the jury was told, two county councillors (one of them Joby Leadbetter) and Dr Percy Hughes, the Medical Superintendent at Barnsley Hall Asylum, were being driven back from a meeting of the County Council. They passed the Queen's Head and turned into Stourbridge Street where, twenty or thirty yards ahead, they saw Blind Jack being led across the street by his little nephew. The child was 'accustomed to walk about with his uncle', his father explained, but witnesses informed the court that the boy and his uncle had stopped halfway across the road on hearing the car's horn and that young Jack had then let go of his uncle's hand and walked right into the car which had swung out to avoid them. Jack Norbury died at the Cottage Hospital within the hour but Jack senior, who had been trapped underneath the car, escaped serious injury.

There seems little doubt that it was a genuine accident and the jury agreed that the running over of a blind man and an infant could not have been avoided. The chauffeur was travelling at about eight miles an hour, he had sounded his horn several times and had done his utmost to avoid the victims. Nevertheless, editorial comment in the same issue of the *Bromsgrove Messenger* focussed on the likely development of 'motor traffic' and the need for debate on speed restrictions in towns.

Jack must have been in his early sixties when he became Jessie Layton's third husband. She had come to Bromsgrove as a young girl in the 1870s to work for the Amphlet family, grocers in the High Street, and recounted in an item in the *Bromsgrove Messenger* how she had fetched water for domestic use direct from the Spadesbourne Brook, only able to carry the pails with the aid of a yoke. With her second husband she had had kept a small lodging house next door to The Mitre at No 11 Stourbridge Street and she continued to run this when she married Jack. In 1934, however, it was condemned by the local council and demolished, and the Wakemans moved into the almshouses in Alcester (now Stratford) Road.

Jack outlived Jesse and died in Rock Hill at the age of 84, sufficiently well known to warrant a paragraph in the paper headed 'Death of "Blind Jack"'. Mention was made of his lodging house as well as his staunch support for the Primrose League at whose concerts he had sung in his younger days.

7 Poverty and the workhouse

In 1936 an old Bromsgrovian recalled, with some regret, a taunting rhyme which he and other non-nailers' children regularly chanted:

> Hammer, hammer, hammer,
> Tink, tink, tink;
> Work all day without any drink.
> Pudding on a Sunday
> Without any fat -
> Poor old nailers can't get that.

With so many nailers in the community the catchment area for Stourbridge Road Board School was bound as a whole to be a poor one. These were the worst off of England's 'white slaves' in the opinion of Robert Sherard who visited Bromsgrove in 1896 to collect material for one of his articles for *Pearson's Magazine*.

The old staple trade had been in serious decline for decades but still employed substantial numbers and by the end of the century 50% of these were women. Whole families, including children

Arthur doesn't mention the workhouse on the Birmingham Road but this photograph of the Bromsgrove Workhouse Fire Brigade, taken in the late 1890s, shows him in his uniform. Standing are Frank Nokes, first left, Councillor Job Leadbetter (captain), fourth from left, Arthur, before he grew his moustache, second from right, and to his right Jim Tarren, the rabbit catcher.

sometimes as young as four, were working long hours and often living in the most abject conditions. When things were at their worst in times of strike many must have been aiming just to keep themselves above starvation level.

Interestingly, Arthur does not mention the four-month all-out strike in 1891/2 (against, yet again, a reduction in wages). Neither he nor his father ever made nails, there wasn't a workshop at the back of his house; but his father and grandfather were nail masters and Arthur must have been aware of the turmoil that winter. Support for the strikers came not only from the *Manchester Sunday Chronicle* but from individuals and organisations all over the country; and Arthur must have seen or known about some of the large open-air meetings that took place, the processions and parades, the visits from VIPs. Perhaps, because of his father's misgivings about the treatment of the nailers by some of the masters and the poor state of the family business when his father died, it was an area of his experience he preferred not to record.

Nailers were more often than not the poorest, but there were others finding it hard to scratch a living, and in this community those on the breadline would have been only too conscious of the awful threat of the 'work'us', the prison-like building on the Birmingham Road (now the renovated Bartlett House) which housed the jobless, the sick, the aged and the mentally ill. The union workhouse, by 1890 serving twenty local authorities, was built to accommodate up to 300 men, women and children.

Some of the children entered the harsh regime with their parents, others were orphans or illegitimate. None were well served by the Board of Guardians which seems to have had a knack throughout the Victorian period for appointing unsuitable masters and matrons. For so long the aim was to avoid any increase on the local rates. So the Board opposed the 1870 Education Act, petitioned the House of Commons against proposals to force poor law unions to pay school fees for all needy children, and campaigned for a school-leaving age of twelve, rather than thirteen, arguing that young earners were needed by their families, that employers were being denied a cheap source of labour and that the burden on the poor rates would be too great.

Arthur makes no reference to the workhouse even though he lived quite close to it until he married and, as a young man, was a volunteer member of its fire brigade. Nor does he mention the children of the workhouse who, in 1881, after years of inadequate teaching in their own classroom, were sent out to the Stourbridge Road School. (A few of the older ones attended Lickey End when Stourbridge Road was full.) A couple of years later the Guardians were ticked off by the Local Government Board and forced to provide the children with capes to prevent them arriving at school drenched and with no dry clothing to change into. Not surprisingly, perhaps, the Guardians reverted to in-house education when the headmaster at Lickey End complained about the effect of the workhouse children's attendance on the rest of his school. They persisted in the face of general criticism and battled with the School Board until 1892 when at last all the children were sent to Lickey End, the infants in suits costing 5/6d, the older ones in suits costing 10/11d. So Arthur would have started school with some of the workhouse children and 'taught' others as a young trainee.

'Guardians' looks like an over-generous title for such a deeply conservative and, at times, stubborn group of men who too often sacrificed the needs of their wards on the altar of low rates. Attitudes began to soften a little, though, towards the end of the century. In 1892 the children were allowed to attend Sunday Schools and join in their annual treats, and the Board even decided to accept a local invitation to all the inmates to visit Gunnett's circus. Arthur's boss, Joseph Tilt, stood for election as a Guardian at the end of the century, one of six candidates for three vacancies. Unfortunately he attracted the least number of votes.

8 The typhoid epidemic

The typhoid outbreak of 1887 was a serious one. It began towards the end of June in the Birmingham Road and in the area behind the Duke of York pub in Sidemoor. In early July Arthur's headmaster noted in his logbook that Edward Kimberley, a monitor, was off with the fever; and a couple of weeks later that fever was seriously affecting attendance. By this time typhoid had also broken out around the workhouse; and Lickey End Board School was forced to close a week early because 'fever, measles and whooping cough were prevalent in the locality'.

At the mid-July meeting of the Bromsgrove Local Board it was reported that pumps behind the Duke of York and in a few Birmingham Road houses were out of order and people were getting their water from 'other sources'. The Birmingham Road occupants were drinking directly from the polluted brook. At the same meeting rather lurid details were given of conditions in some of these latter houses where one of the earliest fatalities had occurred: closets were very close to the back doors, cesspits were located under gravel walks, draining was defective, and the resultant smells were pretty awful. All this was close to the water supply. By mid-August the main problem area was south of the workhouse. The drains behind the New Buildings – where Arthur's father moved his family later the same year – were described as the worst in the neighbourhood.

Bromsgrove's water supply had been a growing problem for a long time. The two main sources of supply were a number of shallow wells and the highly contaminated Spadesbourne Brook. The problem was compounded by widespread ignorance about the dangers of drinking polluted water, and by the Local Board's indecision. Eventually in 1877 the East Worcestershire Waterworks Company was formed and in 1882 the first clean water was piped into Bromsgrove. Unfortunately, in the early years very few took advantage of it: most Bromsgrovians remained unconvinced of the need for clean drinking water, even when the medical officer of health informed them that many of the wells they were using were polluted. It took a long time to accept that pure water was a necessity, not a luxury.

The Local Board's response to the 1887 typhoid outbreak was to get the town's volunteer fire brigade to flush out the sewers south of the workhouse with gallons of water containing disinfectant. Above the workhouse householders were encouraged to flush out their own sewers; and all were advised to boil their water. By late October the Board was confident the epidemic was over.

The following March Dr Carey, Medical Officer of Health, reported to the Bromsgrove Town Local Board that in 1887 ten had died from typhoid, five from diarrhoea, four from whooping cough and two from measles. Most of the dead were children. It is worth emphasising, though, that in all this the town was far from unique.

Joseph Tilt's advertisement in the *Bromsgrove Almanack and Directory* for 1899.

9 Joseph Tilt

Joseph Tilt came from a very old Bromsgrove family. He was born in 1846 to Benjamin and Mary and started his working life as a bricklayer. By the 1870s he was listed in local trade directories as a builder and keeper of the Hop Pole. When his father died in 1880 Joseph, then in his mid-thirties, had already taken over the family business, and he kept the pub until about 1897. Four generations of this well-known Tory family lived close to each other in and around the Birmingham Road and it was here, first in 'the Blackmore' and later on the main road itself, that Joseph had his builder's yard.

Late nineteenth-century directories show that a number of new building firms were established in and around Bromsgrove, a response no doubt to increasing demand for public and private buildings that followed a steep rise in the population (doubling to 20,000 between 1851 and 1901). Most of the seventeen listed in 1909 were probably quite small, most didn't survive the Second World War. Nor did two of the town's much older firms, Tilt's and Read's. By 1900 Joseph Tilt's eldest son Alfred had stepped out on his own, as a 'Practical Sanitary and Ventilating Engineer' offering plans and surveys and the remodelling of draining systems. Not long after his election to the Bromsgrove UDC in 1905, Joseph retired to the house he built on the brow of Stratford Road where he lived until his death in 1914. The name of the business was changed to Messrs Tilt Bros, with three of Joseph's sons, Alfred B, Walter J and Leonard J, in partnership. Leonard, Arthur James's brother-in-law, struck out on his own in 1908, working as a plumber, joiner, decorator and undertaker from his home in the Crescent. He died in 1918 at the age of only forty-two. His wife Amy, Arthur's sister, lived on until 1932 by which time Walter was also dead. Alfred, the senior partner, died in February of the following year.

Tilt Bros was put up for sale shortly afterwards. Presumably there was no-member of the next generation willing or able or to carry on the business. The sales particulars show that the builders' yard in the Birmingham Road stood on a site of over 7,000 square yards, with a frontage of 106 feet, and consisted of offices, showrooms and storerooms, a large galvanised steel shed and three paint and store sheds.

Ethel Merriman, photographed not long after her marriage to Arthur James in 1900.
Both this and the photograph opposite were taken by Arthur W Utton at the
Bromsgrove Messenger Studio.

Arthur James, photographed at the same time as his new wife. Fifty years later Arthur sat down to record some of the people and events that featured in the first four decades of his life.

Arthur had a good memory. *A Cuckoo and a Donkey* was among the songs listed in the Infants logbook that were 'taught by ear'. The singing of songs and hymns was an important feature in the early years and they were copied down word for word in the logbooks.

The inclined gallery was the common solution to the problem of an enormous class of children who had to be packed together in one place so that all could see, and be seen by, the teacher. To some small children galleries must have appeared frighteningly steep – but they provided further 'encouragement' to keep still.

The school, not unnaturally, took a little while to get into its stride and the inspectors didn't mince their words in the earliest reports. In 1881 the infants were described as 'very backward', the girls as 'ignorant', and the boys in Standard 1 as 'thorough blockheads who will need not only good teaching but strong compulsion in attendance'. The teachers, however, soon worked miracles on this seemingly unpromising material. Within a couple of years great progress was made and by the time Arthur started the infants department in particular was building up a very good reputation.

It is worth remembering in these days of mainly co-educational classes that, once they had left the mixed infancy experience behind them, boys and girls were almost always taught separately, they entered the same building through separate entrances and each of the two schools had its own head. Hence the use of the word 'schools' where we would use 'school'.

RECOLLECTIONS

Schooldays

Born in the year 1878 at Walton Road, Norton, Bromsgrove, on December 3rd.

I often heard my parents remark what a severe winter this was. It froze the water in the washing basins which, by the way, was the custom of washing before the coming of bathrooms, a luxury of only a few at that time.

Now, my earliest recollections are of a concert at Stourbridge Road Schools which was given by the scholars each Christmastime. I was chosen out of the Infants School to sing a song, the title of which was *A Cuckoo and a Donkey*, a very old song with a good moral. For this occasion my dear Mother managed to make me a velvet suit, a favourite dress at the time, and to finish this off a large lace collar hanging over the shoulders, and so adorned I remember going on the stage to give my song.

In those days the infants were seated on an inclined gallery, one row above the other, and one had to be careful not to topple over and tumble to the bottom. What a contrast to the present day when nursery chairs are provided, and what long overdue progress has been made in education. In the Infants School you were all taught to knit and sew, and make straw mats of various colours, interesting and pleasing work to the very young. The teachers I remember at this stage were Miss Hooper, Miss Roberts, a sister of Mr Roberts the solicitor in the High street, and Miss Clews who

School fees, usually called school pence, were abolished in Board schools in 1891/2, just before Arthur left. Up till then they were a constant headache for the headmaster. The Board of Guardians, which was responsible for administering the poor rate, not only opposed the 1870 Education Act and the raising of the school-leaving age, but was very reluctant to pay the school fees of poor children – their aim was to keep the poor rate down.

Fees were supposed to be paid on Mondays but in his first week at the school, for example, the week beginning 27 September 1886, Mr Fletcher received £1 on Monday, 2/8d on Tuesday, 2/6d on Wednesday, 3/6d on Thursday and 1/10d on Friday. This, he wrote in the logbook, left him 2/6d short which he paid out of his own pocket and hoped to recover. A year later he refers to the School Board's decision not to insist on pre-payment by the children of nailers on strike – but how were they ever to make up the arrears? Some schools decided to waive fees altogether in similar strikes.

The headmaster had to be on his toes when it came to leaving dates. When Arthur passed Standard 5 he could have left, but he chose to stay on for two more years, presumably with the idea of following in the footsteps of Jack and Amy. But other children who did not qualify by attainment had to rely on the thirteenth-birthday escape route. In 1891, for instance, Mr Fletcher noted that he had resorted to getting copies of birth certificates for several boys claiming to be thirteen but, according to school records, not that old. The certificates confirmed the head's suspicions – and the boys stayed on!

went to Rubery Schools and remained there for many years until she retired.

Moving out of the Infants into the Boys School was a big event and looked forward to by many of us – we thought we were passing from the baby stage into something important. The teachers I remember at that time were Mr Hayward, the headmaster, E G Stanton, E Badger, J Perrygrove, F Martin, O Eades, A Jones, L J Nokes, Frank Jeffrey and W H Duffill. The headmaster following Mr Hayward was Mr C Fletcher. He had a son, Charlie, a cripple who went by the name of Peggy Fletcher because he had a peg so fixed onto the short leg as to give him the height of the long one. And how he did get along on it! It made no difference to him and he was as happy as the day was long – except when he had the misfortune to break it, and this happened often, to his discomfort. Until he had another peg he really was a cripple.

At this time we paid 2d a week, every Monday morning, for our education. I can picture now the teachers and master receiving the money from the fortunate ones who were able to pay; but the less fortunate – and they were many – were sent home and usually failed to return with their 2d. It looks a small amount but when you had a large family, as many did, it was a great sum for parents to find each week, the majority of them poor old nailers and seasonal workers on the land.

To show how poor they were, I remember that when a boy or girl reached Standard 4 he or she was allowed to come to school half-time, one week mornings, the next week afternoons, to make the family income a little larger. These children worked anywhere, some in the nailshop, some at the button factory, and wherever else they could earn a small sum, much to the detriment of their education.

Dinners and soup kitchens were in operation twice a week in the winter months and for the sum of one halfpenny you could eat. The halfpenny bought a cheque paid for at school and given up at the kitchen for your meal. The dinners were given at the back of the High Street where William Corbett had a pop factory, Lickey Mineral Waters. I fetched these cheques many times from Mr Watton who lived just below where Boots the Chemist is now. At that time there were lots of private houses in the High Street.

880 children and 250 adults were provided with bread and soup at the Brewery, and yesterday 1100 children and 150 adults were similarly entertained. Money and bread, oatmeal, meat, and split peas were contributed. (Bromsgrove Messenger, 15 October 1887)

Logbook entries show that the soup kitchen aimed to meet the extreme poverty of the families – in particular, the children – of striking nailers and provide 'a good meal of bread and soup' three times a week. Unfortunately, writes the head, the sheer numbers being served at one centre meant that children were arriving back late for the afternoon, 'considerably interfering with attendance'. (Did some eat up their soup and then go home?)

Early in 1890 a soup kitchen was held at the vicarage 'as in previous years' and about 200 children benefited from a halfpenny dinner each Wednesday; and these cheap meals were still being laid on after Arthur had left the school. Mr E Watton was a member of the School Board and managed the committee responsible for this scheme.

The content of religious education was a source of heated argument and discussion and a major problem for Board schools. The voluntary national schools, like the one in Crown Close, promoted the principles of the Church of England in religious education lessons. But the main source of finance for Board schools, was a government grant, based on results in yearly examinations of the three 'Rs' and on attendance - and sometimes including extra money for teachers with especially good results (so there's nothing new about present government initiatives). Many School Boards up and down the country successfully argued for a nondenominational approach with no catechism and no Anglican prayer book. The subject was debated at national level with Conservatives backing the voluntary national schools, and the Liberal Party supporting the rapidly increasing number of Board schools. This struggle is well illustrated in the minutes of the Local School Board meetings of the late 1870s.

A very tricky situation in all this, as Arthur points out, was the annual examining by a member of the Church of England of children taught on nondenominational lines. They must have been sensitive occasions. In practice, however, the children of Stourbridge Road Board School usually came out with flying colours as diocesan reports show year after year. Perhaps the inspectors were extra keen to avoid disturbing a hornet's nest. Perhaps RE really was excellently taught year after year.

When I was about ten the average boy or girl at school had parents who were nailmakers and I have seen a whole family, father, mother and children – of course, I mean those children who were able to hold a simple iron and make a common nail – working all together under the supervision of father, who would occasionally shout not to blow the fire too much or the irons would be burnt. The nailers reared ducks and chickens and these were housed in the nailshop. At the back end of the nailshop was a cockloft which ran over the pantry, and it was here that the fowl roosted at night. The nailshops were built side to side with a gutter in the centre and the older lads used to climb into these gutters and place pieces of turf on the chimneys. I have seen red-hot irons thrown in all directions by angry nailers, but the lads were always too quick and seldom got caught.

In the Boys School scripture lessons started with hymns sung by the whole school and a passage out of the Bible. We would then return to our class and be given a piece of composition to do on one of the parables – like the Sower or the Good Samaritan – or from the reading we had just heard. I enjoyed these lessons more than grammar or arithmetic. What a pity scripture lessons aren't taught any more. I still maintain that it was the religious bodies themselves who were to blame for not agreeing on a common formula to suit Church, Nonconformists and Roman Catholics. In the end scripture ceased to be taught as it had been in my early schooldays. I think it was the exams that were the cause of much bad feeling because the inspector who came to school to do the examining was a Church of England clergyman and here lay the trouble for the other sects. These recollections on religion in school, I should say, apply only to Board schools like mine and not to the Church of England and Roman Catholic schools which taught according to their own beliefs.

I moved through the lower standards of the Boys School and up to Standard 5, and, by the way, any boy passing this stage could leave school then. Mr Stanton was the teacher, and what a teacher he was, a great burley fellow with a fairly large head. He was nicknamed Bull Head by the class and he did not hesitate to throw the book he had in his hand at whoever was not paying attention.

So the class answerable for the whole school was taught by the barely qualified Ernest Stanton. And, more remarkably, their success was due almost entirely to work done in the classroom. In the autumn term of the year Arthur started, the headmaster's first entry in his logbook was a copy of a notice from the School Board which pointed out that homework was not legally enforceable. It should be given only with parents' consent and consist only of work that could be 'learnt by heart without much labour, or any strain, and without trouble to the parents'. The Board was clearly playing tippy toes in a brave new world opposed by certain sections of society.

Unfortunately, Arthur doesn't mention Fred Byng again, but Gordon, his son, confirms that he remained his father's great pal. Fred won a scholarship to Bromsgrove School and when he left was apprenticed as a gardener at Chateau Impney. Arthur often cycled down to see his friend on a Sunday morning and recalled going into the great glasshouses where such exotic fruits as peaches and nectarines were growing. 'I'm allowed to eat anything that's fallen', Fred would say, before giving the trees a 'helpful' nudge. He eventually took over the nursery business in Churchfields which his father had first established in New Town. (See page 21.)

In case anyone is tempted to smile at the word 'exotic' in connection with fruit now available in every supermarket in the land, it may be worth mentioning that at least some of our options have narrowed. Mr Longfield, 'Fish, Game, Poultry and Ice Dealer', opened his shop in Worcester Street in 1892 and for years included in his wonderful range – on a daily basis when in season – American, English and Dutch oysters, salmon, hare, leverets and rabbits, pheasants, grouse, woodcock, partridge and pigeons.

It was while I was in this class in 1889 that a new order was issued in relation to exams. The inspector could now name a particular class to examine and all the other classes could go home. Standard 5 was chosen, much to our disappointment, and we watched the rest of the school escape while we were left, as it were, on our honour to do our best. And this, I am pleased to say, we did, much to the credit of our teacher. I have a letter Mr Stanton sent in April 1948 in which he recalled this very exam and the congratulations he received from the authorities and inspector on the results. I am glad to say that at the time of writing this (August 1949) he still lives in Chesterfield where he settled after leaving Bromsgrove.

Churchfields Nursery, the Byngs' family business, before the First World War. Arthur is on the left with his brother-in-law Bertram Moore.

I still remember some of the scholars in this class, Standard 5. Fred Byng was one of the best pals I ever had and remained so up to the time of his death. What games we had and what a boxer he was, afraid of no-one. Once challenged Fred was into it right away and if he got one in you knew about it. When we boxed we asked no quarter of each other. Of the two of us, Fred was the master and

Levett and Frank Nokes came from a remarkable family. Their father Levett was a nailer who wrote and published in 1884 a very even-handed account of the state of the nail trade. (See note on page 52.) Levett junior trained as a pupil teacher at Lickey End Board School before taking up his first post at Stourbridge Road when Arthur moved up to Standard 5. Frank started his training at Stourbridge Road in 1892 and became an assistant teacher there five years later. For a while both Nokes brothers were on the small teaching staff. Their sister, Gertrude, a couple of years younger than Levett, was also a teacher. So Levett and Lou Nokes obviously encouraged all three to make the most of the new educational opportunities.

Charlie Troth of York Road in Sidemoor was one of two men in the Bromsgrove area still working at the nailblock in the early 1950s. He concentrated on brush nails and was still making and selling them well into his seventies. He was a lay preacher and stalwart member of the Ebenezer Methodist Church and died in the same year as Arthur.

Comparatively few children are named in the logbook. Arthur Wheeler, on the other hand, has several mentions. Not the headmaster's favourite lad, his passage through the school was 'memorable'. At one stage he is described as the ringleader of most things and frequently in trouble. But he was not a high achiever and it can't have been much fun being kept down. It looks as though he never did pass Standard 5 but had to wait for his thirteenth birthday before happy release.

   Arthur's accident appears less serious in the log entry than in Arthur James's recollections. As he was climbing over the railings on his way into school 'at a quarter before two' (was he late?), he slipped and a spike ran into his leg. He was taken to his aunt's house and then to hospital by his father. He wasn't the first to lose out to the railings, though. Three years earlier another Arthur – Dyers – was attempting the same short cut when he fell and broke his collarbone. Yet there is no reference by Mr Fletcher to the danger of these spiked railings.

Job Leadbetter became a very active member of the community. He served as a fireman with the town's volunteer fire service, and then as its captain for over twenty-two years. He was also a member of the School Board and the Board of Guardians, his social conscience acting as a much needed thorn in the flesh of his more conservative colleagues. It was another member of this family, W G Leadbetter, who wrote *The Story of Bromsgrove* in 1946.

I think he encouraged me by not being too hard at times. However, I sometimes got a good one in but I always knew that Fred would get level in the end. We always finished up the best of pals and ready for the next bout. I shall come back to Fred later on.

There were some clever boys in the class. Frank Nokes, my cousin, did very well at school and became a headmaster in Birmingham. He was a brother of Levett Nokes, another teacher. Arthur Scrivens became a carpenter when he left school, but he was a brilliant scholar and if he'd had the opportunity he would have done very well indeed. Charlie Troth's ambition was to learn a trade, so he told me, but his parents insisted that he was to follow his family into the nailshop. So this he did, and never did anything else; and this he still does in 1949, making a special nail in the same old shop. Ernest Tovey, another good scholar, became a market gardener; and Horace Green went into the teaching profession.

Arthur Wheeler, nicknamed Lion, became a wagon repairer at Bromsgrove Wagon Works. There's an incident involving Arthur that he still talks about to this day. Around the playground were iron railings which were spiked at the top and very sharp. Instead of returning home through the school gate, Lion made a practice of mounting the rails and jumping over to save a few minutes. But he did this once too often and was impaled on the top. He had to be lifted off and was very badly injured. After this the spikes were covered with hoop iron for safety.

Harry Eades worked as a shoemaker at Drury's shoe factory when he left school; Walter Perry was the son of the Methodist parson in Birmingham Road; and George Fardon, W Halfpenny and F Penny were always called 'the $1\frac{3}{4}$ farthings'. Thomas Leadbetter's father kept a fishmonger's and fruiterer's shop in the High Street (still carried on by his sister, Mrs Rushton, in 1950). Thomas's brothers, the late Job Leadbetter, CBE, and Rev W Leadbetter, still living, spent their childhood at this very shop. Alan Watkins's father kept a corn dealer's shop in the High Street, about four doors below where Field's is today. To enter the shop you went up three steps and I spent many hours at his home.

A very nice tribute to Jack appeared in the *Bromsgrove Messenger* on 16 July 1887. The master at Lickey End Board School, Mr J P Okey, reported that John Horton James had died after a week's illness. He described Jack, one of his pupil teachers, as 'most energetic and painstaking', a young man who would be difficult to replace. Such praise for a teenage trainee must have been rare. In stark contrast the inspector's report for that year merely notes that 'J H James' name has been removed from the Register of Pupil Teachers serving in this school'.

Salters Row, Birmingham Road, directly opposite All Saints Church. This row of nineteenth-century cottages was at one time known as Fiddlers Row in recognition of the musical skills of a number of its occupants. The cottages were demolished in the early 1960s.

Typhoid epidemic, 1887

My elder brother, Jack, was a very clever organist and would have gone a long way had he lived. Unfortunately, he was struck down by typhoid in 1887 and died at the age of sixteen. It was a year remembered by many, a very hot summer followed by an epidemic of typhoid fever.

The outbreak was very bad at Norton where we lived. It started in fact at our house, No 1 Walton Place, Walton Road, and went round what was then known as 'the allotment'. There were only nine houses in Walton Road and three houses in Barnsley Road and into the Birmingham Road, and hardly a house missed having a death. I also had the fever and remember being told by my parents after getting well that they were expecting me to go at the same time as my brother. However, I was spared, but in a terrible condition. I was taken to my uncle's at Norton Villas on Birmingham Road where my dear Aunt Sarah helped me to the railings of their house and, by holding me up, taught me to walk again. I was eight years old.

The loss I felt when Jack died is very well described in a poem I learnt at school called *The Child's First Grief*. It goes like this:

Oh, call my brother back to me
I cannot play alone
The summer comes with flower and bee
Where is my brother gone?

It is a beautiful little poem and finishes with these lines:

Oh, while my brother with me played
Would I have loved him more.

That hot summer of 1887 was the first time official records were kept of what was termed a drought. Weeks we were without rain and it was in this period that the typhoid fever struck – and no wonder it did. The sanitation was anything but good. The water was obtained from a pump not far from the WC which, by the way, was an open midden and right next to the pantry. The WC was

Confirmation of the continued employment of the night soil men well into the twentieth century comes from Pershore in the 1930s: 'You had to get home early … If you had been to the pictures and you met the night soil man – the smell was terrible!' The men started their 'necessary' work as soon as the pubs closed (and under the Health of Towns Act this could not be before 10 pm). In Pershore the men's vehicle was known as 'The Honey Cart'.

Arthur put Ivanhoe in inverted commas, suggesting - not unreasonably – that it was a nickname. It wasn't. The children of Elizabeth Smith, single parent, were classically named: Ivanhoe, Horace and Jesse.

Ben Juggins, 'genial, humorously-inclined and kindly', had two almost inseparable friends, Geoff Ward and John Gibbs, and in their younger years the trio could be seen nightly sitting by the brook near the workhouse – just talking.

Jack (John) Kings, son of Noah and Emma, was the same age as Arthur's brother Jack. He was forty when the First World War broke out and could have stayed at home, but he joined up with the 1st/8th Battalion of the Worcestershire Regiment and was a lance corporal when he died on 31 May 1915. He was buried at Calvaire (Essex) Military Cemetery, a few miles from Ypres, leaving a family at Norton Cottages. He was a 'manly' and 'cheerful' person, according to a tribute in All Saints parish magazine, 'for many years as boy and man … an honoured and useful member of our choir'.

emptied by the night soil men, as they were called, and what a business it was. They would start operations at midnight and you could hear them for long enough before they started coming up the Birmingham Road – which was a signal to close your window. Even now, in the mid-twentieth century, this still happens in some outlying districts though not at all in the same way, thanks to improved sanitation.

I can remember the people who lived at Norton Villas when I was recovering from the fever. At No 1 was Thomas Smith, a carpenter and father of the late 'Ivanhoe' Smith, and at No 2 Mrs Taylor, a typical Victorian lady and mother of Mrs Drewitt and Mrs Green, schoolmistresses at Lickey End. No 3 was lived in by my uncle, George James, and Mr Narborough and his wife were at No 4. He was a retired artist who did some work on the panels of his doors that were still there years later when my parents went to live there after leaving New Buildings. Mr B Juggins at No 5 was the first tenant at Norton Villas and remained there until his death. He was the superintendent of All Saints Sunday School for years and worked at the Bromsgrove Wagon Works all his life.

During the typhoid epidemic it was difficult to get any help because people were scared of taking the fever. My parents, though, were fortunate in getting assistance from Mrs Kings whose husband, known as Old Noah, was a nailmaker and worked for my Grandfather and my Father. I could tell many tales about him. His two sons, Tom and Jack, who worked at Bromsgrove Station for years, used to come very nearly every night after work and sit with my brother and me. They never showed any signs of taking the fever.

Jack Kings had a fine bass voice and later on my father taught him to sing with another good singer, Walter Delves. Both were in the choir for many years, but Jack was also a good comic singer and one of his favourites - *Where did you get that hat?* - was always greatly appreciated. Jack was killed in the First World War. He need not have gone but he was one of the Old Volunteers, as they were called then, and nothing would keep him back. Walter, another Old Volunteer, served in the Boer War.

Levett Nokes senior was a nailer who three years earlier had written a short account of the state of the trade including the urgent reforms needed to improve conditions for both masters and men. In *The Mysteries of the Wrought Nail Trade Revealed* Nokes highlighted the poor training parents gave their children and their failure to send them to school; the problems of dishonesty, drunkenness and immorality; the miserable conditions in which nailers lived; the evil effects of working children and women on both family and trade; the failure to unionise; and the shoestring on which most masters and foggers set up. Unlike most Bromsgrove nailers, Levett Nokes looked forward to more nail factories which he thought would overcome many of the trade's problems.

14

introduced into the neighbourhood, which would be the means of taking many out of the nail shops, and thereby relieving that industry of its present over-production."

Juvenile and Women's Labour.

Juveniles, in years gone by, began to work at seven, eight, or nine years of age, as there were not then School Boards and Factory Inspectors to interfere; but now, as there are both, one would think it was altered—and it is a little, but not much. In March, 1883, a man had a daughter who had begun to nail, and neglected to go to school; so the School Attendance Officer went to know how it was. "O," the father's reply was, "her's begun to try to make nails." The School Attendance Officer said that she had better go to school, or else the father would be summoned. The man said she should be sure to go next Monday. When Monday came, he said to himself, "I have a payment to make this week, so she must stop and help to get that," and the following Monday she went to school. As soon as the teacher saw her, she said, "Mary Ann, your name is scratched off;" and when the father heard it, he said that was just what he wanted to hear; so the girl, so far as learning is concerned, is ruined for life, and no doubt, when a woman, will curse the School Board for allowing her guardians to keep her without education.

Most parents put their children on hobs, or shoe bills; these are both shoe nails, and both sorts are easiest to make in the trade. The usual thing is to tell the child,

The beginning of Levett Nokes's section on the employment of women and children in his little book on the nailing industry.

The Birmingham Road community

After 1887 my parents decided to move from Walton Place to try to forget past events. My Father took a cottage in the Birmingham Road, No 16 New Buildings, which was a long row of houses whose occupants were very nearly all nailmakers with their nailshops at the back of the houses. Our nailshop was converted into a scullery and WC but the cockloft was kept (and is still there today). This was all a great change from Walton Place.

Next door lived my Uncle Levett and Aunt Lou who kept a shop and sold a bit of everything – coal, bread, flour etc. My uncle was a very good nailmaker and my aunt hatched out ducks and chickens by the score. I will mention here a not too pleasant thing about ducks and chickens. They had to be fed, and worms were a great part of their meals. These were caught in the early summer after a good rain and at a time when the ducks had to be fattened up for market. My cousin FrankNokes and I used to go out into the gardens at night and catch them – and you'd got to be pretty nimble and quick to do this. At the least sound of walking, as anyone knows, worms disappear and you've got to wait some time before they appear again. We were paid 2d a quart for this slimy part-time work. The worms were measured into a quart can and the pennies, a great deal for us, were gladly received and, more often than not, spent at my aunt's shop.

Nearly all the New Buildings nailmakers worked for my Grandfather and so were well known to us. They were good-hearted and rough folk but very poor, and as well as rearing ducks and chickens to add to their wages they worked on the land in the seasons, digging potatoes and harvesting.

What a sight it was in the Birmingham Road between the Crab Mill and the Hop Pole! The road looked like a farmyard, minus the ricks and straw. Scores of fowl ran in all directions. Nobody seemed to own them and nobody took any notice of them. When a nailer got a new cock bird the lads would wait for an opportunity to drive this newcomer off his beat and into another patch among the old cocks. And then the fun began, a real fight enjoyed by the passers-by – until the owner found out and all the lads went missing.

New Buildings, Birmingham Road, not very long before the cottages were pulled down in Bromsgrove's demolition heyday, the 1960s/70s.

There were some interesting characters among these nailmakers. Thomas Amiss, nicknamed Tommy Kia, I remember perhaps best of all. He would make a habit of visiting us on a Sunday morning about breakfast time, much to the annoyance of my Mother. Yes, and out would come the usual cigar for my Father, obtained by Tommy the previous night at the local pub. These cigars were frequently given to the customers but Tommy didn't smoke. So he found an excuse to bring it round because he knew he would get a cup of tea with a pick-me-up added, which was just what he required, of course, after Saturday night at the local. Tommy had an impediment in his speech, hence his nickname Kia.

Tommy loved children, though he had none of his own, but at times the older ones used to goad him into talking like he did and this made him worse. Tommy kept up his visits to us until we left the New Buildings. Although he was a nuisance at first he became one of us in the end, and if he failed to bring a cigar for Father he would bring us nuts that he'd won in one of Blind Jack's raffles the night before at the pub.

An outstanding feature of this community was that everyone baked their own bread. Ovens in those days were attached to the brewhouse (wash house) along the foad (brick path) away from the house. There was one oven to every two or three houses, so baking was a real communal affair. I remember very well going for the first time to see the oven 'drawn' and all the loaves and lardy cakes coming out, though the cakes were few as people were so poor. Mrs Young lived at the first house opposite the Crab Mill. She had a very small house and a very large family and however she managed, goodness only knows. But then this was true of nearly all the houses in the row. I was pally with her son, Walter. He took to me when I migrated to this community. I spent a deal of time at his home and he very much appreciated coming to ours. His mother was a dear old soul, such a frail little woman but with a heart of gold even though she was so poor. It was there that I first had the pleasure of tasting lardy cakes just out of the oven.

Next door to Mrs Young was Solomon Smith, a rag and bone dealer. He occupied the two houses on the corner, using one as a parts store, and had a shed which stood on the opposite side of the road by the brook on ground now taken in by the churchyard.

'Septuagenarian', writing in the *Bromsgrove Messenger* in the 1930s, describes New Buildings in the 1870s as looking rather neglected and far from 'new' (they had been built a number of years earlier). He puts this down to the poverty of the occupiers – though they were the tenants, not the owners – and comments on some recent improvements to the cottages. A few had even acquired numbers so that they could be found by the postman.

Miss Eliza Hornblower was already in her mid-seventies when Arthur moved to New Buildings. She was still working in 1891 in which year she is listed in the census as a herbalist. In the 1930s another of Miss Hornblower's satisfied customers described her as 'a kind and clever little lady who acted as amateur surgeon to hundreds of men, women and children who visited her when suffering from what we now call "septic" wounds'. Her wonderful ointments, 'surgical' ability and sound advice about cleanliness 'healed most of those who tested her skill'.

As organ blower Billy Lilley once did Arthur's father a special favour. He retrieved a particularly treasured music score given to John James by another member of the Birmingham Road community, John Batchelor Tirbutt, 'professor of music' and organist at St John's. This had been 'borrowed' at some point by Walter Saywell, All Saints' organist. Billy 'stole' it back but always worried that he would be found out.

Yes, you could smell the 'aroma' from this store long before you reached it, and there were rats, swarms of them, which we used to shoot at with a catapult.

I must now pass over the road for a moment to two dwelling houses next to the Crab Mill. The first down was Miss Hornblower's, a dwarf of a lady and very clever at making up potions and ointments. People came from far and wide with their ailments – it was just like a doctor's surgery. I remember being taken to her when I was very young with a bad whitlow which she cured. She was so gentle of touch, this little old lady was wonderful. Next door to Miss Hornblower were Mr Yeats and his son, Fred. Fred had a beautiful tenor voice and sang in All Saints' choir for years with my brother and my cousin, Levett Nokes, when the very first vicar, the Rev A T Massey, was at the church.

Returning to the west side of the Birmingham Road, next to Sol Smith was Mr Strain, the father of Harry Strain who became a tailor and for years, until his death, kept a shop (now The Pantry) in the High Street. The next house was Old Mother Tibber's, famous for her home-made pop which consisted of herbs gathered and brewed up. When sales were slow you could get a quart for a halfpenny. Jack Carpenter was next, a bricklayer who worked first for Benjamin Tilt, the founder of the building firm, and later for Tilt's son, Joseph.

Then came Billy Lilley, a nailmaker and another friend of my Father. He rang the bells at All Saints for a number of years and was also the organ blower. Billy's neighbour was Charlotte Wilson, another nailmaker, and next to her was Charles Price, a nail gaffer who used his house as a warehouse. Then came Jane Williams, an old lady who was what we call a nanny. She took care of the children while their mothers made nails. She also had a lodger, Tom Strong, a great burly navvy.

In the next two houses were more nailmakers, Mr Guest, who had a very large family, and Mr Moses Nokes, a dwarf of a man but good at his trade. Then there was Thomas Manning, a bricklayer's labourer, and next to him William Birch, a labourer and well-sinker, who met with a bad accident in a well when the bucket fell as it was being hoisted and hit him on the head. William's neighbour was William Mole, a bricklayer, a very short stout man, but what

No 16 was near the All Saints Road end of New Buildings and was distinctive because it had a bay window and, together with a couple of other cottages known collectively - before they had numbers - as 'Top Railings', was bounded by a small wall. (See photograph on page 54.) Here in summer, after church and chapel, people would walk up from town and stand outside, listening to the singing and playing.

It is difficult to know whether Arthur's memory is slightly inaccurate when he refers (on page 61) to moving on to All Saints after only a short time in New Buildings. According to the report of the inquest, his mother and father were still living at No 16 when John died in 1911. Was Arthur thinking of his own addresses? He and his new wife lived briefly in Burcot, then in All Saints Road before moving to Norton Villas in about 1902. The other possible explanation is that Arthur's parents lived for more than one period in New Buildings. The movement of tenants from one rented property to another is striking though not surprising.

Walter Saywell was the nephew of Samuel Saywell, headmaster of Bromsgrove College (also known as Saywell's Academy). It began in Blackmore House in Birmingham Road in 1859, but by this time was on its third and final site in New Road, opposite the Cottage Hospital. The college provided a higher level of education for older boys and Walter was the resident music master. He was also the organist and choirmaster at All Saints.

a tradesman! His mates called him 'TheFinisher' and he surely was when he was setting grates and Minton floor tiles. The little bits and pieces when laid looked like a chessboard – perfect! I often watched him at work and it was wonderful to see so heavy a man constantly bending to do such work. His skill can be seen in any of the villas built by Joseph Tilt.

The house of music

I now come to the abode of yours truly, No 16 New Buildings. Though this was a great change from Walton Place we were happy after a while mixing with the lads and neighbours, an experience ever to be remembered. I mentioned earlier about singing a song at school. Mr Henry Clough, a great friend of my Father, was the organist at All Saints in the Rev Massey's time and also, for many years, the organist at the Congregational Chapel. Through this family friendship he took a fancy to me and as a small boy I used to sit beside him at choir practice. Later on, when I was old enough, I joined the choir, though by then Mr Clough had left to take up an important position in Sheffield.

The next organist, Mr Osborne, didn't remain long and was followed by Walter Saywell, another great friend of my Father. Walter composed many pieces of music and it was to this house that he came to submit his compositions to my Father to criticise. Many are the times I have heard Walter say, after playing through the piece, 'How's that, John?', and my Father reply, 'That won't do, Walter. Play it again', and after a few moments shout, 'That's where you're wrong!'. And so the alterations would be made.

I mention this because my Father was almost self-taught. The few lessons he had were given by Blind Solomon who lived at one time at a house next to the Roebuck Inn (on the south corner of the Stratford Road) and it was here that he taught the younger boys of the parish choir. But my father had music in him from head to foot and was never so happy as when he was taking part in anything musical. All his leisure time, and much of his ordinary time, was taken up by his music. My sister Amy had a beautiful soprano voice. She sang all over the district and was accompanied by

Arthur sells himself short here, possibly because he felt he wasn't in the same league as his father who seems to have been a born musician. Music was John's main passion and there wasn't a church or chapel in the area where he hadn't played. Amy recalled an occasion when he was playing the organ at All Saints, weaving one melody into another. A gentleman asked who the organist was. 'I'd love to have a copy of that music. What is it he's playing?' Amy had to explain he was just extemporising. Amy herself had a very powerful voice and was the dominant one of John's children, built, according to her nephew Gordon, like a battleship and always dressed in black satin. Arthur may have felt less gifted but when he was young he mastered the clarinet, flute and piccolo, and later played in several dance bands.

Arthur, Ethel and their eldest child Hilda in the yard of No 1 Norton Villas in about 1902. Hilda was born in All Saints Road but shortly afterwards the family moved to Norton Villas where they lived for thirty years.

my Father. The performances, by the way, were given free. They did it for the pure love of music.

It was in this humble New Buildings abode that Amy took charge of All Saints choirboys' Christmas carol practice and here that glee parties were trained. I can remember the crowd of lads and grown-ups who used to gather outside our house to listen to these training sessions – which were concerts on their own. My Father had a deal of trouble at first with some of the listeners, but in the end we had no problems at all and people would ask: 'When's the next do?'

My own musical abilities, however, were not much, although I loved anything musical.

We weren't very long in New Buildings. We were soon on our way to All Saints Road and finally to Norton Villas – and still Walter Saywell and the musical parties came for free tuition from my Father. I often heard my Mother say: 'Don't ask them. The barrel's out!'

Blind Jack

Next to us at No 15, as already mentioned, was my Uncle Levett's shop, and then at No 14 Harriet Young and her brother, Ned, both of them nailmakers. At No 13 there was George 'Sweat', real name George Nokes, another nailmaker who got his nickname, I think, because he was always hot and bothered. He had a large family and I knew his children well – Joe, George, Ted, Charlie, Walter, Harry and Lil. All of them made nails as soon as they became old enough. I particularly remember young George. He made a nail called a *sparrable* which was about $\frac{5}{8}$ of an inch long and used in making heavy boots. I have seen him knock off twenty-four at one heat using double irons. When he left school he became a bricklayer and later on a builder and contractor. George was a good tradesman, a good singer and a good footballer. His brother, Joe, also a bricklayer, was later a foreman at Tilt Bros and then at J and A Braziers. Ted, another good singer, was a plumber and painter before starting out on his own; Harry and Charlie were bricklayers, and Walter, another painter, went out to the USA.

The local paper reported an increase in drunkenness for the year11900: 114 cases had gone before the courts. At that point in Bromsgrove's history the population of 16,000 had a choice of seventy-three licensed premises. But it wasn't just the men who fought. In 1936 a 'Modern Septuagenarian' recalled a fight he had witnessed as a boy in about 1870 involving two drunken women who punched, scratched, swore, pulled out hair and rolled about in the Strand, all in broad daylight.

Arthur's references to friends and acquaintances who had emigrated are an accurate reflection of what was going on at this period in our history. Until 1890 poor families were encouraged to move to the colonies by their local Poor Law Unions who dangled before them the carrot of assisted passages. Others, not in such dire need, took the decision for themselves, but all set off with the hope that their far-flung destinations would provide a better life. Between 1880 and 1914, the peak period, nearly 13 million left the UK The most popular destination by far was ex-colonial America which, unlike most of the colonies, provided plenty of opportunities for townspeople, as well as much higher wages. Next in popularity was Canada, followed by Australia, New Zealand and South Africa.

The Board of Guardians, the executive body of the Bromsgrove Poor Law Union, was initially reluctant to pay the poor to emigrate, but when times were hard and work was difficult to get it found the assisted passage a useful solution. In 1873 it was even prepared to accede to a Canadian government request to suggest the names of orphaned young girls 'willing' to emigrate. It was a short-lived and probably unsatisfactory arrangement.

A number of the extended Crawford family, mentioned on page 65, emigrated to Australia, paying their own way and making their own arrangements since these were qualified men – a teacher, a builder, a printer. A feature of the local newspaper in the decades either side of the start of the twentieth century is the accounts of those who had made the move, most of them very successfully.

I mention the different trades the brothers went into because in their youth they all made nails. Joe got married very early while still an apprentice and went on making nails every night after he finished bricklaying to add to his small wage. But great credit is due to all the Nokes brothers and to their parents.

Yet more nailers lived at No 12, Mr Rowlands' family, at No 10 was Thomas (Kia) Amiss, at No 9 Joe Bony Dipple –he really did look all bones – at No 8 Mr S Clarke and his son, Walter, and at No 7 Samuel Kendall, a very surly fellow, always ready for a fight. These fights in the road between rival parties were accepted as part and parcel of their behaviour while the drink was in them.

Mr Wakeman at No 6, nicknamed Ninny, had a very large family. Some of his children moved to Scotland and some to the USA, including 'Boser', a plasterer. Old Ninny made nails and lived to a great age. When I worked for Tilts the builders we did a deal of undertaking and I remember taking Ninny's coffin to the house and hearing his old wife, who was very ill, asking for him. But before he was buried she too died and Ninny's funeral was postponed so that the old couple could be laid to rest together.

Mr Erne Kendall at No 5 kept a small shop and also sold milk. He was a brother of Samuel, the surly fighter, but a different man altogether. Later he took on a small farm in Sidemoor and into his old house moved Mammie Lou and Mr Wakeman, the parents of Blind Jack. (They had previously lived at No 16 which we now occupied.) Mr Wakeman had a pony and trap which he hired out for a day or a half-day, as required, and many are the rides I had in that little trap later on in life. Their son Jack was not born blind. People said his blindness was the result of paddling in the local brook.

Anyway, he grew up to be a well-built man, as strong as a horse, and he was a great friend of my Uncle and Aunt Nokes, so I saw a great deal of him and got to know him very well. If any bother occurred at the local pub it was Jack who was always fetched, and woe betide anyone who got into his grip. They felt as if they were held in a vice and out of the pub they came! I have a recollection of Jack walking all the way up the Alcester Road, along Pikes Pool, and back home down Burcot Lane, all for a bet. But there was one thing he did not like and that was the snow. It put him off his

The little boy's death must have affected Jack Wakeman very deeply and no doubt he would have found it impossible to deliver papers for a while; but he did not give them up for ever, as Arthur suggests here. Gordon James remembers Jack delivering to Norton Villas, where he lived as a boy, in the late 1920s and early 1930s. He recalls a great mountain of a man with a voice 'like a bull's' – not a man to be messed with. There was never any danger of not hearing Jack's shout, 'Post-a-Mail'. It was deafening. And Jack, he remembers, would wait at the edge of the kerb for a helping voice to shout 'All clear, come over!'.

There were several lodging houses at the top of the town. Their guests were largely itinerants in search of seasonal work who possessed just enough money to save themselves from the workhouse up the Birmingham Road. The best lodging house would provide mattresses, the most basic would offer only 'lean-overs' which were long fixed rails where men and women could rest their arms as they slept standing up.

The plaque bearing Jack's name is still there at the Hop Pole, on the bench just to the right as you enter the pub.

Jack Wakeman was not the only blind man to stamp his personality on Bromsgrovians. Joe Phillips, known as Blind Joe, used to cry out public notices around the town centre and rose to at least one big occasion (the ending of the First World War) with verses of his own. He was the obvious choice in the 1880s for shouting out the news about the coming 'invasion' of the Droitwich Salvation Army Corps who felt called to establish a presence in Bromsgrove. Blind Joe was instructed to preface each announcement with the word 'Hallelujah!' three times, but he was a member of St John's Bible class and the vicar advised him at the end of the first day that shouting out 'Hallelujah!' was irreverent. The word was duly omitted, but the Army marched from Droitwich, sang heartily, held a lively meeting in the evening, recorded eleven conversions and prompted a small prophecy: ' … they have come, and they will not leave till the Judgment Day.'

'Blind George' – George Dyer – attended the National School in Crown Close when he was a middle-aged man. For a number of years he would sit in an easy chair by the schoolroom fireplace and select boys to read to him from a book or a newspaper. Most of the chosen enjoyed the break from school routine and they learnt something because George was very keen on clear and intelligible reading and could explain the meaning of words. Every Friday George went into school for an hour to accompany the boys' singing on his fiddle.

bearings. Jack was a great pigeon fancier and he could tell his birds just by the sense of touch. It was wonderful to watch. He also liked football and was taken to the matches played on Wells Lane and afterwards on the present ground. There he would listen to the comments of the crowd as the match went on and in the evening at the Hop Pole would argue with the customers when they were discussing the game, remembering all the moves of the different players just from what he'd heard.

Every Saturday night in his younger days Jack sold nuts at the pubs, starting at the Crab Mill with a basket and his measure and dice. The customers would make up a party and pay him so much for a raffle. Then he would shake the dice and the winner took the lot. He continued all the way down into town, taking the pubs as if his eyes were open. You could hear him say 'Beg pardon' if he happened to bump into anyone, but all made way for Jack.

For many years he delivered the evening papers all on his own, but in the latter part of his life, when traffic increased, he had the assistance of a small boy, the son of Joseph Norbury, one of Jack's great friends. Unfortunately, this small boy was killed taking Jack across the road. After that Jack gave up delivering papers.

He married later on in life and kept a common lodging house in Stourbridge Street, opposite the East Worcestershire Waterworks Company. He was a wonderful character and being blind was no worry to him. He was more awake than most of his pals who had their sight. At the Hop Pole Inn Jack had a special seat which was always given up when he went in. Anyone visiting the pub will notice the brass plate with the name 'Blind Jack' on the side of the seat that used to be his own. The plate is taken over by incoming tenants or managers and charged as a fixture – '1 Brass Plate and 2 screws ... 3d'. May this ever remain. Even if a new pub is erected I hope this brass plate will be taken care of.

At No 2 New Buildings was Mr W Crawford whose son, William, became the organist of Brisbane Cathedral in Australia, and at No 1 Mr Webley, a brother of the jeweller who kept a shop in the High Street. Arthur Webley, the youngest son, was at Stourbridge Road School and was the last to carry on the business.

In 1891 the Tilts had almost taken over this area around the Hop
Pole: Joseph Tilt, the builder, was at the pub itself, his mother and brother
were next door, another brother and his large family were the other side of
the pub on the Birmingham Road, and his three eldest sons were on the
opposite corner of Blackmore Lane. Interestingly, in view of Arthur's
remarks, Mary Tilt at 72 was also sharing her house with three young
grandchildren. She was the former publican at the Hop Pole, so probably
felt the kitchen was still hers.

The two cottages were put up for sale in 1913, along with the Hop Pole.
James Tarren's rent was £9.15.0 a year and for this he, his wife and five
children got a 'brick-built and slated dwelling' consisting of a kitchen,
pantry, sitting room, three bedrooms, a brewhouse, garden and tapped
water. The rabbit- and rat-catching business can't have been too bad.

Bath House where Joseph Read lived was next door to the Primitive
Methodist Chapel, Hephzibah. There were two Joseph Reads in the latter
decades of the nineteenth century, the elder short and stout, the younger
'tall and angular and a prominent Independent', according to a man who
played with Charles, the latter's son, in the 1860s/1870s. At the end of the
nineteenth century Read's was almost certainly the longest surviving
building firm in the area, established as early as 1824. Like Tilt's, it
survived well into the twentieth century.

Blackmore and the Hop Pole

Finishing with the New Buildings and passing over the road, the Hop Pole was kept by Joseph Tilt, a very shrewd businessman who carried on his building and contracting firm here. All his children were born in this house, Alfred, Walter, Leonard, Arthur, Elizabeth and Rose. The family also occupied the house on the opposite side of the road in the New Buildings which had been Charles Price's nail warehouse. Alfred had a very serious illness which prevented him from carrying on his trade as a bricklayer, but he took up architecture for his father's firm which he pursued for many years. He designed the two houses in Birmingham Road, now the Council Offices, where his family moved after leaving the Hop Pole.

Moving down Blackmore, on the left we come to two cottages. The first was occupied by Mrs Mary Tilt, Joseph's mother. She lived with her son, Samuel, to a great age and was a tough old lady. I remember her so well because my Uncle Fred Richardson lived next door with his aged parents and she was a terror to his children. She broke her leg when she was in her seventies but recovered and was still able to wander up to the Hop Pole for her pint of home brew which she drank in the kitchen there till the day she died, much to the disapproval of Joseph. I could relate many things about Mrs Tilt, some not so good.

Later on, Jim Tarren, a well-known rat and rabbit catcher, moved into this house, and lower down the road were the Perrys, the Dolphins, the Sandfords and the Scrivens. It was in the Blackmore that Joseph Tilt stacked his bricks and building material, quite a builder's yard in fact. For years he had no special yard and all the business was carried on from the Hop Pole until he opened what was later known as Tilt Bros, now a garage.

He was not the only one to use Blackmore in this way. Joseph Read, another builder, who lived in Bath House, stacked his bricks on the opposite side and we had many games with these bricks when no-one was looking.

Leonard Tilt was a pal of mine and we both served under William Weaver, learning the joinery trade at his yard in the Strand. We had our own workshop in the yard of the Hop Pole where we spent

Arthur started at Lickey End at the beginning of 1892, and in October of that same year his sister Amy qualified after five years as a pupil teacher there. Amy carried on at the school but Arthur failed his exam the following year and left in September 1893 to take up an apprenticeship in the building trade. The family connection with the school was even closer. Jack was also a pupil teacher at Lickey End until he died from typhoid. Dora, the youngest of the four James children, was the only one not to embark on teacher training.

Supporting three pupil teachers must have been quite a sacrifice for John and Emma. The salaries were a pittance. Jack started his apprenticeship on £12 a year, about half of what he might have earned in the very badly paid nailing trade.

Amy was just finishing her third year as a pupil teacher when this report was written. Jack, had he lived, would have been nearing the end of his training.

our spare time at night, and where I saw a great deal of the pub life. Len would take me up into the clubroom to play bagatelle and it was here that the Saturday night Money Club was held. Each member held a share into which he paid weekly for a fixed period. Members who wished to receive their shares before the due time could put them up for sale to the highest bidder at a Saturday night meeting.

The method of sale was a tallow candle and pin. After dues were paid the candle was placed on the table and the pin inserted at a distance it was thought the bidding would go. The candle was then lit and at the fall of the pin the highest bidder took the share. I watched this happening many times.

Out to work: men and boys at William Weavers

After leaving Stourbridge Road School I became a monitor at Lickey End School and taught Standard 1 for just about a year.

> Birmingham Road
> Bromsgrove
> October 26th 1892
>
> Dear Gentlemen.
>   As my engagement
> with you expires at Christmas,
> I should be glad to know if my
> services will be required at Lickey
> End Girls School after that date.
>   If so, I should be pleased
> if you could raise my salary to
> £16 per annum.
>   I hold a 2nd Class
> Queen's Scholarship, and good
> recommendations from present
> and past mistresses.
>   An early answer will

Amy was one of the better qualified teachers, having passed the Queen's Scholarship exam which enabled her to go to a training college for a year and get her certificate. She did get re-engaged at Lickey End Board School.

Fred Edmunds, only four years older than Arthur, was appointed monitor in 1889 after passing Standard 7 at Finstall Boys' Board School, and was still training when Arthur arrived at Lickey End. It is clear from a letter to the Board, asking approval of this 'nice quiet' lad's appointment, exactly why the head was keen to get him: 'He is musical which is of great value in a school of this sort.'

Charlotte Pearcey, aged 71, was attacked with an axe on 13 January 1893 while her husband lay upstairs suffering from bronchitis. She died later that day. Her assailant was identified as Aime Meunier, married to an English woman and living in central Birmingham. Within a fortnight Meunier was arrested in Brussels and the jury at the Worcester Assize in July took only minutes to find him guilty. He was hanged at the prison in Castle Street.

Apart from Braziers, which closed in 1990 after 140 years, all William Weavers competitors of the nineteenth and early twentieth centuries have long ceased to operate. Weaver plc was established in 1865 by William Weaver, the son of 'Weaver the Milkman' of Townsend Farm. The quality of work, its location close to the hub of the country's road network, and the fostering of long-term relationships with employees and clients are three of the factors which have contributed to the firm's expansion into a £40 million construction group that operates across England and Wales. In the very early years Weaver partnered other local firms for some of the bigger projects. With Braziers, for example, William Weaver built several Board schools; and Arthur makes clear that until the turn of the twentieth century Weaver and Tilt undertook a number of jobs together.

Charles Britten (see also pages 86-87) at some stage set up on his own, possibly about the time Joseph Tilt retired. Certainly between 1906 and 1912 he was advertising his building and contracting business in Stourbridge Road.

The headmaster was Mr Henry Drewitt, his wife, Elizabeth, was headmistress and her sister, Mrs Agnes Green, was head of the Infants, quite a family affair. My sister, Amy, was also a teacher at the school. The teaching itself did not appeal to me, rather it was the lessons and study before and after school. But this all left little time for recreation. You had to be at school by 8 am for the master to inspect your homework and give you instruction until school started at 9 am. I got on very well with Mr Drewitt and he was disappointed when I gave it up – and so were my parents.

The teachers I remember by name were William Irish, Enoch Waldron, Ada Nokes and L Kendall, but the one I remember most at that time was Fred Edmunds who came from Aston Fields and was also the organist at Lickey Church. Fred married Miss Bridgman from Townsend Mill and went to live in New Zealand. At the time of writing this (February 1950) Mr Samuel Jukes, organist at the Baptist Church in New Road, received a letter from Fred saying he had composed an anthem which he was sending to the Lickey Church to be sung by the choir.

I was at Lickey End when the terrible murder of old Mrs Pearcey was committed. She had a small shop at the corner of Alcester Road and Shiply Road selling odds and ends. She was murdered by a Frenchman who was caught (on the Continent) and paid the penalty at Worcester Gaol.

After leaving Lickey End School I was apprenticed to William Weaver, the father of the present William Weaver whose firm is now a limited company in the Strand. It was usual then to have one apprentice to each man employed and for a very good reason – we were used as labourers to push the handcarts from job to job. In those days you were apprenticed for seven years and had to pay your employer a £10 premium. You started at 2/- per week with a rise of 1/- each year. No holidays, only the official bank holidays.

What a life it was. For the first three years we were simply domestic donkeys. True, we had one horse and cart which was used for moving the timber from Bromsgrove Station to the yard, but the rest was done by apprentices harnessed to the handcarts. I remember Charles Britten and me having to push the handcart all the way up to the Lickey Church area to a house where we had some work – and this, by the way, was in the winter. When the

Among the fifteen nail manufacturers listed in the Bromsgrove area in *Ryland's Hardware: A Complete Directory of Midland Manufacturers* (1894) was 'Henry Parry & Co, The Crescent Nail Works'. It was on the verge of closing.

Edwin Coxell, the 'old' gentleman, was not much over sixty at this stage and managed to carry out his duties as registrar, relieving and vaccination officer, and collector for the town area within the Poor Law Union, as well as school attendance officer. He also found time to make the operating table, three other tables, chairs and bedside chests for the new Cottage Hospital.

Walter Gilbert (page 73) was the headmaster of the school, in fact, appointed in early 1898 when Arthur was nineteen. It is not clear whether the Bromsgrove Guild of Applied Arts was the brainchild of Gilbert or of the Art School Committee that appointed him, but it was set up at the end of that same year, quickly developed into a successful commercial concern and went on to achieve a worldwide reputation for the quality of its work. Arthur must have been very conscious of the guild's work even at a local level. Evidence of its output can be seen in All Saints, Arthur's parish church, and the guild's bronze tablet in honour of those who lost their lives in the First World War was made for Bromsgrove Secondary School, Arthur's first job as foreman at Tilt Bros.

Joseph Guise (page 74) died in 1895 and was buried in Finstall cemetery. Hard work obviously suited him. For many years he worked long hours at the button factory before taking on Caspidge Farm, near Pikes Pool. He was at least ninety-one before he gave that up and moved nearer the town.

New Road Institute, the present library, was built all the timbers from the Assembly Hall roof were planed up by hand and pushed on the handcart from the yard and onto the site. I often complained to my parents about this but to no avail. It was all considered part of your training.

William Tranter was one of the joiners at Weavers, a short man with a nanny beard, and a very strict man to work with. He was a good tradesman and had been in business on his own before coming to Weavers. He it was who did the Assembly Hall roof. I once worked with him on a roof at a house in Stourbridge Road, and I recollect I was on my way home and had not got far when he called me back. He had noticed a few nails under the roof on the floor and instructed me to go round the whole house and pick up all the nails, adding, 'This will be a lesson for you when working for me', and indeed I never forgot, whether I was working with him or anyone else.

John Turton was another good joiner, and if you could please John you really had done a good thing. He was a very hasty man and did not hesitate to cuff you under the ear for the least error. John was the first technical instructor at night classes which were held at The Crescent, New Road, in a disused nail factory. It was built by Mr Parry of Catshill but was a failure because the nailers would not take to a factory – they preferred their freedom with their ducks and chickens, and so this became the first technical night school for woodwork.

I spent all my free evenings there after working from 6 am till 5.30 pm. The class had all ages in it, including some in their sixties, and there were many who didn't follow the trade but just did it as a hobby. John Potter was one of these, a very good gardener who went by the name of Gentleman John. And there was Mr E Coxell, an old gentleman who lived in the High Street at a private house that is now Barclays Bank. He was the registrar of births and deaths but was also a good amateur woodworker. I remember him making two notice boards for the parish church. They are still there today (13 February 1950).

At the technical school there were also classes for ironwork and copper beating. The instructor was Mr Gilbert, a very clever artist who worked at the Bromsgrove Guild when it was known all over the world for the fine work it turned out. In later life, after leaving Bromsgrove, he designed the reredos in Liverpool Cathedral, a lovely piece of work.

Roger Penrice was also a skilled joiner. At that time Weavers did a great deal of undertaking which was carried out under the personal supervision of the old boss. So it had to be just so. The coffins were taken either on a handcart or in the pony trap, and the apprentice went along to look after the pony – which I did many a time. Mr Joseph Guise was a farmer in Pikes Pool Lane and a familiar figure in the town in his white smock. After giving up farming he went to live in Conway Road where he died at the age of 101. The boss and Roger did the job of putting him in and as usual I went along to hold the pony, but was surprised when the boss said to me: 'We shall tie the pony to the gatepost tonight and you shall come in with us. This may never happen again in your lifetime, to say you helped to put one in at so great an age.' This was the first time I had anything to do with putting anyone in and I always remember Roger when I think about it. As the two of them were arranging the shroud the boss said: 'I cannot find his arm!' 'It's all right, boss,' Roger replied, 'he's only got one.' You see, Mr Guise had lost an arm many years before his death.

William Wall was a good joiner and wood turner and also a man who had a good opinion of himself. In conversation he always tried to sound superior but failed badly because he used words he never understood. He used to write the word as it was spoken – kake for cake, for instance. Each man had a material board to record the amount of timber used for the week on his jobs and Bill would make his out so: '2 dosen screws, 2 ft 6 in x 5 ft 1 in English Oke.' We apprentices had a good laugh at his board.

Bob Wilmot was an outside carpenter and one who worried a great deal about the state of the country, forever saying, 'What a state the country is in!'. Everyone who worked with him referred to him by that catchphrase. John Wall was a very tall man and good at his trade. He was a peculiar sort of fellow to work with, though. One of his favourite sayings was that if a man was killed he did not die. He would argue for hours if you tried to question his way of thinking – and then what a state he got into. He didn't realise we did it for amusement, just to get him going.

Joseph Pearce, always known as Sopit, was a short man with a red beard. He was a good wood turner but spent all he earned at night in the local pub – he really did 'sop it'. He drank away a row of houses he owned in the Strand, he just couldn't leave the beer alone. William Davis was a pal of Joseph's, a good joiner and a decent sort. But Will's failing was also beer. It was said that he was jilted by a girl early in life and this had brought him to the gutter. Will and Joseph would work for a while and then take to the road, singing hymns and begging alms. Yes, they were two decent tradesmen in their young days but lost all respect for themselves in the latter part of their lives.

Then there were the apprentices. John (Jack) Duffill was the head apprentice when I started and what a lad he was. He liked a chew of twist and a glass of beer when he could get it. I remember in later years Jack was sent to the Ford House Farm to do some repairs in the cottage where the bailiff lived. An apprentice by the name of Edgar Albutt was sent with Jack and their work took them into where the bailiff kept his barrel. Sure enough, the two of them sampled it. In the end, however, they were unfortunate because the bailiff caught Edgar just before they finished the job and accused them of emptying his barrel. He gave them the option of buying another one or being summoned.

Jack took no notice but the bailiff got to know that Edgar's father was a man of wealth – and he was. Billy Albutt was the town crier but made a fortune by money lending. He also had a stall on the Market Square, now done away with, where he sold fruit and a good class of sweets. He was the only man, in fact, that the boys from the grammar school could buy from. But he misused this privilege by lending the boys money and when it was found out it was taken from him. The bailiff knew he was all right, that Jack had put Edgar up to pleading he had nothing, and one morning Billy came into the yard to see Jack about paying his share. Jack did not budge but remarked: 'We shall both of us have to go to gaol, then.' This did poor old Billy and he paid up to save Edgar, much to the amusement of all of us and of the bailiff who got another barrel out of it. I don't think Jack and Edgar drank a great deal but, still, they were caught.

Harry Wright came from Stoke where for years his father kept the

The photograph above of the Birmingham Road yard of Tilt Bros, shows Arthur (left), Mr Canning, a carpenter (centre), Leslie Kings an apprentice (right) and an unknown apprentice in the background. It was taken in the 1920s and the suits and clean shoes suggest the men knew they were to photographed, probably to mark the completion of this particular order for Mr Jones, a coal merchant in Sidemoor.

Tradesmen often bought just the chassis of this very popular vehicle, the Model 'T' Ford, from a local supplier and a very crude wooden seat had to be fixed to enable the driver to get the wheels, engine and bonnet to the local builder's yard where the body would be built to specific requirements. The two headlamps would only light up when the engine was running. Power for these and the ignition was provided by a number of magnets attached to the engine's flywheel and had to be 'excited' by cranking the engine – no battery, no self-starter. So oil lamps were provided for the side lamps and also for the rear lamp which had red glass facing rearwards and clear glass on the side to illuminate the number plate.

Leslie Kings moved on to the carpentry shop at Longbridge and ended up as maintenance carpenter at Rubery mental hospital.

*Navigation Inn. He was full of devilment and the old boss was
always reporting him to his father. He would occasionally bring a
slice of venison with him, for instance, and cook it over the fire at
breakfast. And what a smell! You could cut it with a knife. Harry
did this more for devilment than anything else and I have witnessed
many stormy scenes at mealtimes.*

*Harry Kimberley was an orphan whose parents had died in 1887
during the typhoid epidemic. He was educated at the Blue Coat
School in Stourbridge and apprenticed by them. Harry had a very
hard life during his apprenticeship and I have known him not have
enough to buy a pair of laces for his boots. He went on to do well
though. After his apprenticeship he moved to Bournville Estate
which was then being developed and from there he went into the
factory and became foreman over the building department.
William Birch, nicknamed Stocker, was a dwarf of a chap who lived
in the New Buildings. He always seemed to be under the weather
and stuttered very badly.*

*All these apprentices served seven years. I was the only one who
didn't and for this reason. Harry Turton, John Turton's son, started
after me, and his father, being the leading man at Weavers, never
paid a premium. Harry was also receiving a shilling a week more
than me – which did not go down very well because a shilling was
a great deal then. Then when I was nineteen years of age my old
boss died and this put an end to my apprenticeship as far as my
indentures were concerned, but Mr Weaver junior could have agreed
to take me on under new conditions. My conditions were that I
should receive the same amount of wages as Harry Turton, but the
new boss would not listen to my proposal and this situation went on
until I told him I should leave. So he sent for my Father, but I
fought this out. In the end my Father said he'd had done with it
and he'd finished with me, and left me to do the best I could. This
was just what I wanted. William Weaver refused to give up my
indentures and remarked to my Father: 'John, you will regret this.
He's losing the last two years of his training.'*

*But I didn't regret leaving because after working the first week
at Joseph Tilt's my wages, instead of 7/-, were 20/- and I thought I
was a millionaire!*

20/- was about the going rate for a craftsman at the end of the nineteenth century. So Arthur, not out of his apprenticeship, was delighted to be paid as a fully trained adult. Generally, though, wages in the building industry were low and remained so for many years. At least Arthur was not a bricklayer, subject to the vagaries of the weather. It wasn't just poor nailers who benefited from free meals. Soup kitchens were also laid on for building workers when severe frost led to lengthy stoppages.

Joseph's bids for building the first three Bromsgrove Board schools were never quite low enough and each time he was pipped at the post by Braziers. He put in a joint tender for Dodford Board School with William Fisher, a builder and coffin maker in the High Street, but without success. He did manage to win the contracts for the cleaning and repair of the schools at Dodford and Stourbridge Road, but not until 1881 did he build his first school when he and Fisher offered the lowest tender to the Stoke Prior School Board for the building of a new school at Aston Fields in the parish of Finstall. Joseph's links with the Aston Fields area were strong: in 1886 he built the clothing factory in Carlyle Road and in 1897 the parish hall, which also served as the Sunday School. Other work included the workhouse infirmary (1885), the police station (1890), the Wesleyan Chapel in New Road (1883) and Bromsgrove Secondary School and Pupil Teachers' Centre (1912).

William Fisher (see page 86) went bankrupt and ended up working for Joseph Tilt.

On to Tilt's and back to Tilt's

I worked for Joseph Tilt for many years. This was after Tilt and Weaver decided to work separately. Together they had done some very good work, Tilt the brickwork and Weaver the woodwork. When I started at Tilt's all the work was done by hand. We had no machines except a circular saw which was turned like a chaff-cutter, and hard work at that, not much quicker than using an ordinary ripsaw. But labour was cheap and when we had a deal of sawing to do two labourers were sent to turn the old saw. What a revolution I witnessed while working there – planing machines, bandsaws, mortise machines, spindle machines, tenon saws and scriber machines. They did away with the very hard work which in my apprenticeship days had all to be done by hand. I question whether the present-day apprentice could do the work we were expected to do without the use of the machine.

After working some time at Tilt's I decided to have a change and went to Barnt Green to work for David Edwards, a great burley Welshman but a good employer. He lived in the end house next to the station road and built all the houses up to the railway bridge by the Victoria Hotel, now converted into shops. At this stage I lived at The Mount in Burcot and it was quite a journey in the winter months.

The workshop was full of Welshmen and they were a clannish lot, but the locals kept them in their place! I was fortunate in having a mate from Hereford who had a bit of Welsh blood in him but was a good one to work with. We were given all the best jobs, much to the annoyance of the Welsh. Every day we were all allowed to have a pint of beer at 11 o'clock in the morning and another at 3 o'clock in the afternoon. One of the labourers would fetch this in our tea cans from the Victoria Hotel. Smoking, though, was strictly barred and anyone found doing this was open to the sack.

After meals out came the cards and David was never so happy as when he had a hand along with the men. This only happened, we noticed, when his wife was away on holiday. I have seen him call on hands that were impossible to get and so build up a nice kitty which the others were keen to win. But they seldom did because suddenly out would come his watch as he shouted, 'It's time you

March 15th 1912

Mr. Arthur William James has been employed by Messrs Tilt Bros as Foreman of Joiners throughout the erection of the above new Schools, I have had abundant opportunities of observing his conduct. He is most courteous and obliging, being also strictly sober, He is a thorough good workman, and can set out work well, he is punctual, persevering, and capable, I believe him to be a trustworthy man,

J. Turberville
Clerk of Works

Mr Turberville's unsolicited reference for Arthur (see page 83). In the 'golden' age not everyone was a perfect speller but the handwriting was nearly always clear and often stylish.

devils were at work!', and at the same time out would go his feet sending the kitty all over the floor. He enjoyed this every time.

We worked ten hours a day all through the year and it was very hard work in that shop, every bit done by hand. When I recall the conditions under which we worked I often wonder the place wasn't burned down. We strained our eyes working by the light of paraffin lamps which were hung up over our benches.

After three years the work at Barnt Green fell off and I was expecting the sack. One morning on the way to work I met Joseph Tilt, my old employer (this, incidentally, before 6 o'clock in the morning). He was also on his way to a job in Barnt Green and said he would be pleased to see me back in my old job. I considered the offer and decided to take it. David Edwards was annoyed. After explaining that in view of the shortage of work I had expected to be stopped, not being one of his own clan, and so had taken up Mr Tilt's offer, he said: 'I may be a Welshman but they'd have gone before you.' He asked me to stay on and even left my job open in case I wanted to go back. I appreciated the offer and whenever he met me afterwards he would stop and talk, no matter where. I remember walking down the High Street years later with Alfred B Tilt, who became my employer after his father's death. David was driving down to the bank and he stopped his horse and called us over. 'You stole him off me, Alfred!' he told A B. But both men took it all in good part.

In charge

My return to the old firm was a welcome change. It was nearer to my home in Burcot and by this time machinery had been installed which meant easier work and more rest for the bones. We did some very good work around Barnt Green and the Lickey but our wage packets were very small and remained so until the First World War. Things did get better then but we were never paid our worth.

I worked my way up at Tilt's and in the end was foreman for many years. My first job in charge was Bromsgrove Secondary School, not a bad one to handle for a start. The brickwork was done by Joseph Nokes (George Sweat's son), a real tradesman. He could

Bromsgrove Secondary School and Pupil Teachers' Centre (now Parkside Middle) was founded to provide boys and girls with a minimum of four years post-elementary education. It was started at the Art School in New Road on 6 October 1905 and the first headmaster, Mr F A Hibbins, was appointed a couple of months later. He remained in charge until his retirement in 1940.

The date on Mr Turberville's letter shows that Arthur is referring here to new buildings opened at the bottom of Stourbridge Road in 1912. He may also have worked on the 1921 enlargement but he could not have been involved in the developments of the late 1930s: Tilt Bros had ceased operations several years earlier.

Mr Hibbins steered the school through several changes, including the pre-Second World War change into the County High School. After retirement he went on living in the same Victoria Road house which Joseph Tilt had built, and until his death attended every speech day. Former pupils remember his portly figure, his huge black-and-white moustache and his sheer presence. His son Ted taught at Watt Close (now St John's Church of England Middle School) and his daughter married the deputy head of her father's school, Mr O T H Williams.

lay a brick and do the setting out of any building, and he set the pace for the other bricklayers. Under him worked Jack Wensley, one of the best men ever to lay a brick.

The clerk of the works, however, was Mr J Turberville, a very shrewd and strict man who was also clerk of the works at Barnsley Hall Asylum. It can be imagined how I felt under him, in charge for the first time. His job was to inspect the material (no sap, no knots) and the construction, and I remember him coming into the shop when we started to make the joinery, seeing the work in progress, and turning to me: 'I suppose you've not got anything under the bench out of sight?' 'You are at liberty to find what you like', I replied, 'and condemn it before we waste our time and workmanship.' This had Turberville nonplussed for a moment. 'That's not what I expected', he remarked. 'I will take your word, my lad, and no doubt we shall get on well together.' And we did. When the school was finished he sent for me before he left and to my surprise gave me a recommendation he had written on the way the work had been carried out. It applied only to the woodwork and joinery and I still have this today.

Mr Hibbins was the first headmaster of the Secondary School and he was very interested in the construction of the building. He used to call every morning and walk around the site, looking forward to the time of completion. Before this new building the school was housed in the School of Art and in part of the Institute, now the public library, and hadn't many scholars at that time.

A rather strange thing happened in connection with the building which was kept quiet from the public. Mr Gadd, the Bromsgrove architect, got out the plans in the first place and work was started on them. We'd got as far as laying the foundations and making the joinery when suddenly the work was stopped. Another architect, Mr Rowe of Worcester, was appointed and new plans were got out which we worked to.

Mr Rowe was a real gentleman to work with and we did quite a deal under him – the children's home in Stourbridge Road was one job, Evesham Schools was another, and there was work at Worcester and all over Worcestershire. He became the county architect and remained so up to his death. He was a lieutenant in the First World War and quite a few of Tilt's men had served under

The Cattle Market Tavern was on the south side of Church Street, just up from the cattle market and the annual horse fair. In 1884 the tavern was owned by Joseph Fitch (who also owned the Dog and Pheasant) but by 1896 the innkeeper was Samuel Davis.

The first advertisement for the newly named building firm of Messrs Tilt Bros appeared in the *Bromsgrove Almanack and Directory* for 1906. 'Late Joseph Tilt' refers to the business: Joseph himself had merely retired.

him; so when he had finished his inspection he would gather them round and enjoy talking about all their doings in France. This reminds me that one of the last jobs I did for Tilt Bros was the lychgate at All Saints, given by Alfred Tilt after the First World War. His father, Joseph, had been a bass in the church choir in his earlier days, along with Alfred Smith (of Smith and Russon, the estate agents) who had a beautiful alto voice, and H Snell, a tenor, who was a saddler and had a shop in Worcester Street.

As it happens, two men I have already mentioned from my early days at Weavers, Charles Britten and Jack Turton, were joiners on the school job. Jack had just given up the post of woodwork instructor and when he started I well recollect him saying to me: 'Arthur, do you remember when you began at Weavers and I used to give you a kick of the ass for not being attentive?' 'Yes', I replied, 'I do - and now it's my turn.' ' You ought to thank me for what I did – and you can kick mine if you want.' I *was* very thankful for what Jack had done for me. He was happy under me and carried on working for Tilts until the day he died.

I remember one little story about Jack from my apprenticeship days. We were working at the Cattle Market Tavern, now the Labour Club, but then a popular house at fair time, catering for people connected with horse dealing and the like. The landlord decided he wanted small cubicles in the pub's attics, but it was going to be a rushed job and there was not much time before Fair Day on 24 June. I was sent to assist Roger Penrice and Jack, and just as we started the landlord came up and said to Jack: 'I want it finished the day before the fair.' 'You find the beer', Jack replied, 'and you'll get what you want.' I was kept busy carrying the material up two flights of stairs to the attics, no easy job, with Jack shouting at me all the time to hurry up. I got one shout from Jack to find a bucket. 'What do we want a bucket for?' I shouted back. 'You bring it up and then you'll see. And no back answers.'

The landlord had been supplying Jack and Roger with as much beer as they could drink and it was now having its effect. But frequent runs down two flights of stairs to the lavatory would make the landlord suspicious. So Jack overcame his difficulty by using the bucket and pouring the contents onto the roof. I'm convinced the more beer Jack drank the quicker he worked – and the job was finished to time.

Charles Britten was a very different man. Jack drank enough to sink a boat but I can't remember Charles ever taking a glass of beer. When he was eighty he fixed a new flagpole on the tower of All Saints Church and at the time of writing (28 August 1950) he is still riding a bike down the High Street. Charles is the only man alive who worked at William Weavers when I started there and there's one little incident neither of us has ever forgotten.

We were sent to Townsend Mill to repair the floor over the waterwheel. The wheel, by the way, was considered one of the best in the district and it took very little water to drive. Charlie somehow dropped a tool inside the wheel, so we both went outside and got through the doors and into the wheel. In picking up the tool he got himself on the wrong side of the wheel which began to turn. I can see him now – he came up on one of the arms and shot out into the doorway. I wonder he was not killed. Charlie thought someone had started the mill, but of course it was his own weight that had done it.

When I started work at Joseph Tilt's, after leaving Weavers, I worked with William Fisher, a very good joiner. He was crippled in his fingers from chalk rheumatism and how he held the tools was a marvel to me. I did all the heavy work for William but this was fully repaid in free tuition. He would show me anything I wanted to know about how to set out and do a job. It was strange that William Fisher was having to work for Joseph Tilt at all because earlier on he had been a master joiner working on his own. He'd also done work in conjunction with Tilt and it was Tilt and Fisher who had built the infirmary at the old workhouse in Birmingham Road. But William went bankrupt and in the end finished up as a journeyman under his old partner.

Another old carpenter was Alf Fielding. He was always under the weather, and always worried about his work, especially if he had to set out and do the job on his own. Many times he would say to me: 'Arthur, have you ever thought and thought till you could not think at all?' He was working on some cottages once at Warwick Terrace on the Old Station Road, laying floors in the bay windows. But he made *too* good a job of it, fitting them so tight that he pushed the brickwork in the bay in all directions. The boss, Joseph Tilt, was as keen as a hawk, nothing missed his eye, and he appeared on the job just as this was happening. 'You'll make me scratch all the hair off my head, the damage you're doing!' Not knowing what he meant, Alf replied, 'You can scratch it off your b----- ass if you like', and of course was sacked at once. He went on to live to a great age and was in his nineties when he died a couple of years ago.

George Hoomans, another joiner at this time, was known as 'the pikelet puncher'. His parents kept a small shop in the Strand, next door to William Weaver, my first boss, and there they made their own pikelets. At work the men were always telling George they knew he was the one who made the holes in the pikelets. Later on, George left the building trade and kept the Cattle Market Tavern. He took over from Sam Davis, the landlord who had found Jack Turton enough beer to get his job done quickly. Sam never did return to the licensed trade; but George is still alive, now eighty-four, and still draws a pension for service in the Boer War where he fought alongside Walter Delves.

Joseph Tilt

After he left the Hop Pole Joseph Tilt lived at what are now the Council Offices in the Birmingham Road. The building was started with the intention of becoming the new Hop Pole Inn and Hotel, and has cellars under the whole of the front part, but the plan never matured. Tilt thought that the brewery company would jump at the offer, but it didn't. So he built an adjoining workshop and offices and lived there for many years until he finally retired from the trade. His sons took over from him and renamed the business Tilt Bros.

Joseph was very punctual and would open the yard gate every morning and stand there waiting for the men to come in. He was never properly dressed, though, with his collar and tie in his hand and his boots unlaced, but he would stand at that gate until we were all in. We had to be in the yard by 6 o'clock in the morning and if Joseph thought any of the men were late he would turn

The four children of Arthur and Ethel James photographed in about 1919: Hilda, left, Gordon, centre, Phyllis, right, and William (Bill), in front.

them back till 9 o'clock. 'Ah, lad, it's gone six a minute and the others are half-way there', was one of his sayings, meaning that some of the men who had nothing to take on the handcarts had already left to walk to the jobs they were working on. If the job was under a mile from the yard you had to start work at 6 o'clock. Over that distance you had to be on the way and have walked a mile by 6 o'clock. If you were taking a handcart you started from the yard as soon as you were loaded up and you pushed this back in your own time after leaving off at 5.30 pm.

I remember my Uncle Fred Richardson telling a tale about a handcart. He worked some of his time for Joseph Read, the builder who lived in Bath House, next to the Methodist Chapel (and the man I have already mentioned who stacked his bricks in Blackmore Lane). One day my uncle was pushing a handcart back from a job with his two sons on the front. They were coming down the hill by Townsend Mill, and at that time there was a draw-in on the road where people used to give their horses a drink. He turned the handcart into the pool and upended both his sons. He really liked to tell this tale, he was all for devilment, but Joseph Read threatened to have him summoned because, he claimed, Uncle Fred had tried to drown his sons.

A very familiar figure at this time was a man named Sammy Rea, a carter employed by Joseph Tilt. In his time he carted thousands of bricks from the Linthurst brickyard with the help of his old horse that he loved. Sammy never drank tea with his meals but he always had his pint of beer with his breakfast from the Hop Pole. One morning when he was getting this one of the apprentices, Edgar Albutt, got some cobbler's wax, warmed it, and put it on the seat by the fire where Sammy sat. It was a cold morning and a good fire was burning – and when Sammy tried to get up he was stuck fast to the seat.

But I remember a very much more serious incident involving the old mortar mill and Hubert Dipple. The mill was driven by a steam engine and had a large wheel connected between the engine and the mill. One day Hubert got caught in this and was nearly killed. The wheel kept taking him round and round until someone finally heard him shouting out and stopped the engine. He never came back but went instead to work at the Bromsgrove Wagon Works, built himself a bungalow in All Saints Road and lived there until he died.

Hubert's place was taken by Joseph Flower, as good a servant to a master as you could find. Joe was born in Bewdley and worked on the Severn tunnel for various contractors all over the place. I don't remember what brought him to Bromsgrove but he made it his abode and died here in 1947, aged eighty-four. He was a great believer in herbs for the cure of ailments of the body. In the spring he would take a walk and collect them, then brew them and make them into medicine. He was especially keen on hayrife tea, but I remember talking to him about all sorts of herbs. I have happy memories of Joe – he had a cheerful disposition yet knew what it was to rough it.

How strange that two such well-known builders, Joseph Read and Joseph Tilt, are now out of existence. Both were flourishing firms and had sons to carry on, but they let the businesses simply die out. The work they did, though, remains.

Joseph Tilt had a very hard life when he was a boy. I have heard his wife say that in his young days when dinnertime came round he was sent to play in a field opposite the workhouse. This was his 'dinner'. He vowed that if ever he was fortunate in life he would buy the field in remembrance of this. He did buy it and intended erecting houses on it. But, after making a very good job of building a brick wall along the brook, he fell foul of the Council who said he had encroached on the course of the brook and as a result must pay a nominal sum each year for doing so. In the end this business prevented him from carrying out his housing scheme. The plans had already been prepared but Joseph was soured by the whole episode and turned them down. It would have been better for the ratepayers of Bromsgrove if he had gone ahead, though, because Joseph sold the Council the field and the council houses built on it after the First World War cost nearly £1,000 each.

Joseph Tilt also rented the field along Victoria Road which is now the Rovers Football Club. At the bottom end was the old mortar mill and on this field too Joseph had his yard before he transferred it to the Birmingham Road. Each year the field was put up for mowing and in the spring the lads he used to employ – and there were many – were sent to pick up the stones. Just before leaving-off time

Joseph would walk across to the field and meet the lads coming back. 'Have you picked up *all* the stones?' 'Yes, sir', they always answered. 'Ah, lads, then go and pick up a few more till 1 o'clock.' And back they went.

I remember he used to keep peacocks in the yard on the Birmingham Road field as well as a flock of guinea fowl which roosted at night in an elm tree. The birds used to wander all over the road and how lovely they looked in their full plumage. But at moulting time he didn't get his hands on all the feathers! What a contrast, though. Fancy seeing the peacocks and guinea fowl wandering over the main road today.

Joseph built a private house on the Alcester Road, Mount Pleasant, and would never have given up work if he hadn't become an invalid in his later years. Even so, he never missed coming to the yard and giving his instructions, telling people what to do, just as he had done when in charge.

He also had a farm in Shendley Fields where he cut down some very good oak trees and had them sawn and stacked in the yard with instructions to make his coffin out of some of the timber. I was the one who made it and witnessed the end of Joseph Tilt, an unforgettable character to those who knew him.

The Dragoon Inn

One can hardly believe the progress in transport. All we had then were horses and carts, hansom cabs and brakes. The brakes were used to take parties to the Lickeys, Clent and the Habberly Valley. You sat facing each other and had to be careful to hang on to your seat when going down a hill and turning corners. Going up a steep hill was easier - you had to get out and walk so as to ease the horses.

To get to Bromsgrove Station a bus, drawn for years by horses, ran from the Golden Cross in the High Street. A familiar figure to be seen on it each morning was Mr George Juggins from the Dragoon Inn who sat on the box with the driver. And a fine looking old gent he was. He always sported a flower in his coat and was

Joseph Tilt built a number of houses in the area. In Bromsgrove, for example, he was responsible for some of the new dwellings in All Saints Road; in Redditch and Greet, Birmingham, he built rows of terraced houses.

'Shendley Fields' - nowadays spelt without the 'd' – (see previous page) was in the Shenley area of Northfield, the Birmingham suburb which until 1911 was part of the county of Worcestershire.

The old Dragoon was an eighteenth-century coaching inn. Mr Juggins was in charge throughout the 1890s and into the twentieth century and all that time Elizabeth Jane Crewe was selling her beer from much more modest premises. But the inn was not big enough to cope with the increase in population brought about by the advent of the train and subsequent development and in 1905 it was replaced by an art nouveau-style building erected by William Weaver. Robert Vernon, now the proprietor of the Dragoon Hotel (to give it its correct name) was keen to let the area know about the new place and inserted a one-off advertisement in the *Bromsgrove Almanack and Directory* for 1906. It had been, he explained,

entirely Rebuilt
Refurnished and fitted up with
All the Latest Improvements

It could accommodate cyclists (a increasingly important facility), and it now had a bowling green as well as livery and bait stables. More recently the pub has been renamed the Ladybird Inn.

always neatly dressed, complete with his light-coloured bowler hat. The fee for this ride, incidentally, was 2d each way which was considered dear.

The old Dragoon was a small place, now turned into dwelling houses and a butcher's shop. I remember when I was an apprentice being sent there along with John Wall to repair the floor in the bar under the counter. John told me to keep the doorway full of rubbish for a while once he had taken up the floor. I only found out the purpose of this later. John was after lost money under the floor, but George Juggins also knew about the possibilities and spoilt his little game. He pushed his way through the door and remained there until all the rubbish had been taken out. Then he picked up the lost coins – but not quite all of them. John was very annoyed and when dinnertime came – in front of George Juggins – he sent me with his tea can to fetch a pint of beer from the outdoor at Aston Fields, kept at that time by Mrs Crewe, and drank this and not the Dragoon's beer with his dinner

THE MANUSCRIPT FINISHES HERE

94

Index